A FIGHT TO THE
DEATH

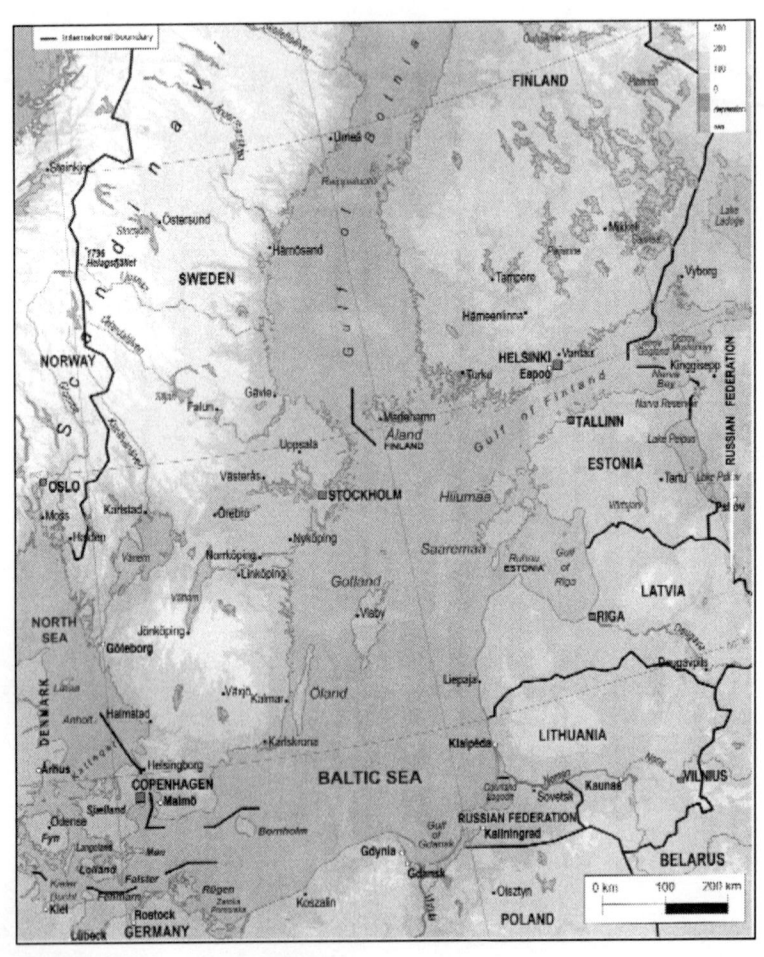

MICHAEL GUNTON

A FIGHT TO THE
DEATH

Copyright © 2009 Michael Gunton

The moral right of the author has been asserted.

Apart from any fair dealing for the purposes of research or private study, or criticism or review, as permitted under the Copyright, Designs and Patents Act 1988, this publication may only be reproduced, stored or transmitted, in any form or by any means, with the prior permission in writing of the publishers, or in the case of reprographic reproduction in accordance with the terms of licences issued by the Copyright Licensing Agency. Enquiries concerning reproduction outside those terms should be sent to the publishers.

Matador
5 Weir Road
Kibworth Beauchamp
Leicester LE8 0LQ, UK
Tel: (+44) 116 279 2299
Fax: (+44) 116 279 2277
Email: books@troubador.co.uk
Web: www.troubador.co.uk/matador

ISBN 978 1848761 551

British Library Cataloguing in Publication Data.
A catalogue record for this book is available from the British Library.

Typeset in 11pt Book Antiqua by Troubador Publishing Ltd, Leicester, UK

Matador is an imprint of Troubador Publishing Ltd

This book is written as a tribute to the bravery of Polish sailors during the first weeks of the Second World War. Although fictitious it is based on the true story of the Polish submarine 'Orzel' (Eagle).

I am grateful for the advice I received in writing the book from the late Marek Oldkowski who served on the 'Orzel' during its service with the Royal Navy. He was drafted to another ship shortly before the submarine sailed on its final patrol.

EAGLE – CREW

Captains	Henryk (taken ill)
	Andras (was 1st Lieut)
First Lieutenant	Andrzej
Lieutenants	Tomaz
	Piotr
Engineer	Jersey (lieu)
Gunnery Officer	Mucha
Warrant Officer	Kazik
Chief Petty Officers	Tadeusz
	Stefan (coxswain)
	Jacek (bosun)
	Ryzard
	Artor
Petty Officer	Marcin
Wireless Operator	Slawomir
	Jan
Cadets	Eryk
	Marek
	Yarwin
	Kacek ('doctor')
Gun Crew	Grzegorz
	Tabbert
Seamen	Guayne (Leading seaman)
	Dasay (Leading seaman)
	Lukasz (Leading seaman)
	Waldeman
	Jake -1st class
	Henerey
	Hreinski

PROLOGUE

Silence.
Total silence.

A silence so intense it made the nerves tingle. It was a silence intensified by the background noise and violence of explosions of bursting bombs and shells set in a framework of flashes of light and clouds of thick black smoke. Hell was being re-enacted in what, only hours before, had been a peaceful world basking in the cool September sunshine.

Five chalk-white faces stared intensely at the small, circular, perforated disc of the speaker in the black box in front of them, willing it to produce a noise, any sort of noise, any noise that showed that there was life at the other end.

"Keep trying," said an authoritative voice. Slawomir, the wireless operator, sighed deeply and looked to the heavens for patience. He knew it was a waste of time, but it was more than his life was worth to tell that to Captain Henryk. He twiddled the knob for the hundredth time with the same result. Nothing.

Some twelve hours before, the Polish submarine *'Eagle'* had been at its Baltic base at Puck, Gdynia The crew had been with their friends and colleagues, laughing and joking even though they knew that war was imminent. But their idea of war was based on stories of the 1914-18 War where battles were engaged mainly in muddy fields. There had been a tremendous loss of life among the troops, but it had been fought in battlefields and was little more than an inconvenience to the ordinary civilian.

"Does not look good," said the grim faced Captain in a massive understatement. "Either our set is broken, which is unlikely, the set at the base is kaput, or the base itself has been destroyed. Judging by what we saw earlier I think the last alternative is the most likely."

The news was received in stunned disbelief by the anxious crew. Everything was happening so fast. They were being quickly brought to a clear understanding of what modern war was about. Two days earlier the German battleship *"Schleswig Holstein"* with its eight 28mm guns, had paid a 'courtesy' visit to Gdansk (or Danzig as the Germans called it) with much pomp and ceremony.

Early the next morning it had moved 400 metres further up the river and opened fire on a small Polish military base called Westerplatte on the opposite side. Then dive bombers had arrived and attacked the naval base at Gdynia, of which Puck was part, and begun its total destruction. The Post Office at Gdansk was attacked and hotly defended by the staff until the Germans sprayed it with petrol and then set fire to it.

In the overwhelming panic at naval headquarters the *'Eagle'* had been ordered to sea to patrol Gdansk Bay. What they saw as they sailed away, and then learned that these attacks were being repeated elsewhere, made them understood the force of a sudden early morning invasion supported by a massive, well equipped overwhelming army of tanks and men. The implications of what the Captain had said slowly infiltrated the consciousness of the 54 men aboard.

Fear was the overwhelming emotion. Fear, not for themselves, but for their families and friends in Poland. A Poland that was being destroyed by the Germans. Their country was being torn apart, communications were crumbling, and they were fully aware that their own army was in no state to fight back, and their air force was practically non-existent. Their immediate reaction was that they would hold out, but in their hearts there were no doubts about the outcome of the war.

But as they came to this inevitable conclusion their subconscious minds were considering the future. Some were uneasy that however much they wanted to fight on they would not be in a position to do so. Others feared what would happen to them if they fought on and failed. The rest, probably the majority, had a more heroic vision in which they saw the Captain as gallant leader of a team of fighters engaged in a lone battle against the enemy, dependent on no-one, seeking out the enemy in a series of individual battles, and destroying them.

They had no idea how they were going to fight on, or whether they had any future at all. It was up to the Captain.

"Despite what is happening," Captain Henryk declared, reading their minds and looking determined and sure of himself, "we will continue to do what we were ordered to do, go out on patrol and sink German ships. We will then work out how we are going to continue the fight."

His statement was greeted with a murmur of acquiescence diminished only by sneaking doubts.

The crew was a close-knit combination of professional sailors such as Lieutenants Piotr and Tomasz and engineer Jersey; experienced non-commissioned officers, Tadeusz, Marcin and Stefan, first class seamen like Jake and Guayne and the volatile Dasay. Three devoted and enthusiastic, Officer Cadets, Eryk, Marek and Yarwin. and a bunch of enthusiastic volunteers, and plain hard working lower ranks, with a single purpose, all aiming to make sure that the *'Eagle'* was the best submarine in the Navy.

But all these men, joined in a determination to fight the enemy, had their individual fears and thoughts, their minds wavering between the difficult task facing them and events in

Poland where their families were facing unknown horrors.

First Lieutenant Andras, the second-in-command, was struggling with thoughts about his pregnant wife. The engineer Jersey knew his father was dying, leaving his young sister all alone. Senior Lieutenant Piotr had left harbour with a 'Dear John' letter in his pocket announcing the end of his marriage. Another lieutenant faced the problem that the man who had stolen his fiancée was now a member of the *'Eagle's'* crew. Another was concerned that his family of innocent country folk would be overwhelmed by the Nazi forces. A seaman was fighting with the horrifying discovery that he was a claustrophobic, facing a life shut up in a steel box under the ocean. They all had their own problems.

Yes, they told themselves, we will continue the fight, but how the hell will we do it? Without bases, without a refuelling source, without aircraft support, with no part of the Baltic Sea out of range of aircraft, in a sea with vast areas of shallow water totally inadequate for submarines, the future did not look too bright.

"Return to your posts. Set a course for the patrol area, half speed ahead," the Captain ordered briskly, his face took on a look of cheerful confidence, his strong jaw firmly set.

* * *

ONE

Unknown to the officers and men of the submarine the most affected person was the horror-stricken Captain himself. He had no fear of the contest ahead, the dangers and the difficulties which would face the lone submarine. He had every confidence in his crew of determined, mostly experienced, men. His fear was intensely personal as for the past few days he had been ill, a stomach pain which he himself had diagnosed as probably appendicitis, but which could be something worse. The order to leave the Puck basin in the face of the German attack had pre-empted by only an hour or so his decision to report to the base hospital, as he had a strong feeling his illness could be fatal. It certainly felt like it.

The intensity of the action and the events following the receipt of the sailing order put his personal matters out of his mind. Now, with the lack of response from the base radio and the prospect of sailing the Baltic Sea alone, without support, made the difficulties of the future seemed insurmountable.

The immediate task was to put aside his personal problems and work out what to do next. He was pleased by one thing, the German attack had ended the unnerving uncertainty which had plagued the recent months.

It was clear his first duty was to obey orders and patrol the

Gulf of Gdansk and sink any German ships that were unfortunate enough to be around. He would stay submerged until dark, surface and re-charge the batteries.

When night fell he took the submarine up into a cloudy night, the moon sporadically obscured, after checking through the periscope that all was clear. The sea was fairly benign, slightly choppy, but with a gentle swell. He was happy about that because he was fully aware that the Baltic could turn nasty, very quickly, and without warning.

His mind turned to recent events, and he recalled that he knew something like this might happen after the Germans broke the Munich Agreement and completed their occupation of Czechoslovakia earlier in the year, with only muted objections by Britain and France. Logic had told him that their next target would be Poland.

"Are you alright?" The question came as a shock because he had been so engrossed in his thoughts that he had not heard anyone come up behind him. It was Andras who had joined him on the bridge.

"Yes, fine," he replied. Andras looked sceptical. He was well aware that his Captain was not well. He had seen him holding his stomach and wincing when he thought no-one was looking.

"Fine bloody mess this is," the Captain opined.

"We can hardly claim it was a surprise. I expected this when they finished the war in 1914 with the Treaty of Versailles, a cock-up from start the finish. It's a true saying that the foundations of the next war are always laid in the peace treaty that ends the last one.

"Making Gdansk a free city, with the useless League of Nations in charge, and giving us economic rights was the catalyst which started all this," Andras suggested.

"That's true, but what made it worse was the war with Russia in '21 which gave us parts of Belorussia, and the

Ukraine, and enabled us to become a proper nation and therefore a threat. It made us the target for any other nation with aggressive ambitions, and Europe's full of them," the Captain said to himself as much as to his close friend. "It doesn't make what has happened now more acceptable."

"No," Andras replied, "but it sort of confirms that the real reason for this attack was that the rest of Europe did nothing, and allowed the Germans to get away with their occupation of Czechoslovakia. Once they got away with that, we were in their sights."

They both remembered that immediately afterwards the Germans made demands that Poland agreed to returning Danzig to Germany as well as yielding important rights in the Polish corridor, the strip of land between Danzig and the German border. Of course, Poland rejected those demands. They had been given moral support by Britain and France who jointly promised to aid Poland in the event of German aggression. Both men knew that this invasion meant an end of the country as an independent nation.

"It's ironic," the Captain remembered, "Do you remember that five years ago President Pilsudski had suggested to the French and British that they should pre-empt German aggression by invading Germany there and then. Hitler was not yet in total control, there were still Germans who remembered what war was like and what it had cost their country. The German army was a bare 200,000 men and therefore not too big to handle.

"He said that the French should march into the Saar, and the Rhineland, and disarm the Germans. At the same time the Poles would disarm them in Silesia, Pomerania and

East Prussia. The British, he thought, would be all talk and no action.

"He reckoned that a small victorious war was better than a large disastrous war, and there was a lot of sense in that. The

British, he suggested, were terribly moral and would voice indignation, but do nothing. They were busy making money trading with the Germans and that would be their major consideration. The French, he thought, had no morals and would go along with the plan."

Andras nodded agreement, but said nothing.

The two men stood silently looking at the horizon and watched what seemed like the utter destruction of Gdynia and its surrounds. Even at some distance the noise brought home the reality of war. What was once a small fishing village, and had become Poland's much needed port and naval base was no more.

* * *

Outlined by the flashing of explosions and the pink glow of burning buildings on the horizon the two officers presented a tableaux which always amused the men, with both respect and affection. The Captain was a thinly built 1.8 metres, and the First Lieutenant a squat 1.5metres. When explaining an order to a colleague the messenger would always conclude: "that's the long and the short of it."

The fair haired Captain exuded dignity and authority. From a wealthy family, and well educated to the highest standards, he gave orders clearly and precisely knowing that they would be carried out to the letter and not misinterpreted. He never felt it necessary to subsequently check whether they had been carried out. If, on a very rare occasion, something went wrong, he did not jeopardise his dignity by losing his temper or getting angry. "Make sure this does not happen again" was his strongest rebuke, but the implied threat was unbelievable hell.

In sharp contrast, the short and compact Andras was a human missile of unflinching resolution, nothing was impossible. Full of energy, despite many stresses and strains, he had an enthusiasm which was infectious and brought the best out in the crew. He was equally sure that his orders would be carried out. His tone of voice, steady, but with a subtle hint of terror, ensured that a mistake was not repeated. Both men were revered by the crew and this was the strong foundation of an enthusiastic, professional team.

* * *

Andras went below to check what was happening, leaving the Captain alone, apart from two lookouts concentrating on their tasks. His mind turned to his wife Dorota.

What, he thought, would happen to her? Married for ten years, but with no children, she had been constantly trying to persuade him the give up the Navy and join her father in the family manufacturing business. It had been going on for some time and he had begun to consider the possibility. But he really did not want to become a manager in an office, spending his life making soulless engineering equipment. He loved the sea and its freedom and variety. He loved the Navy and its discipline and comradeship. But he loved Dorota and wanted to spend more time with her. Now he had no choice. Dorota would be alone with her father, her mother having died some years before, but that wasn't a problem as they got on well together. Now, in a shattered country ruled by the vicious Nazis what future was there for them?

He was afraid for himself, of course, but primarily for her. Of what might happen to her if the happiness which had been an essential part of their marriage was finally destroyed and she was lost somehow in the ruins of Poland. No more comfortable evenings at home, no jokes with and against each other, no conversation during which each knew what they other was going to say and, importantly, no nights of passion.

It was important that she should be safe. And there was, he realised, his own physical condition which could make any thoughts about his future irrelevant. Would he live to see the end of the war?

He looked again at the horizon. Was there more they could have done? Should the *'Eagle'* have attacked the German battleship? He knew this would have been impossible because the warship was deep in the harbour, and the water too shallow for the submarine to attack submerged. On the surface it would have been blown out of the water before they could fire a shot. But it would have been good to try.

The battleship should, of course, have been bombed, but he knew that the Polish forces had been completely unprepared for the attack despite the fact that everyone knew what the Germans were going to do. The Polish army was at half strength, thanks to Britain and France instructing them not to mobilise in case it upset the German. The air force was almost non-existent, and the aircraft they had were out of date. The Navy had been slightly more alert and had despatched several ships to sea and to Britain before the attack started. He sighed heavily. The future of the *'Eagle'* was in his hands. If only he felt physically up to it.

* * *

The submarine continued its journey across the calm, flat surface of the sea. The crew on watch below in the sultry heat, strained and worried. Few of them spoke, each had their uncertain thoughts about the future. Those at their posts were tensely awaiting the next order, which they expected to be an emergency dive.

"I said something funny was going to happen," said Officer Cadet Yarwin.

"You didn't say anything of the sort and it's not funny,"

interrupted Grzegorz, a man who was a stickler for accuracy. Yarwin ignored him.

"I went several times to Gdynia, in August, to deliver messages and then on the last one I had a strange feeling of foreboding. The dockyard was dead quiet and nothing was moving to disturb the water, which was like a mirror reflecting everything on the shore. It changed when the *'Schleswig Holstein'* entered harbour with a bunch of destroyers to anchor about 150 metres out," Yarwin added, pleased to be in charge of the conversation.

"Did you hear that crap Hitler put out?" The wireless operator, Slawomir shouted.

"I don't see how we could've, we haven't got a bloody radio," said Grzegorz.

Like Yarwin, Slawomir ignored the interruption. Known as "Fatty" to his friends because he was extremely tall and very thin, he was constantly complaining that he never put on weight. He was pleasant, friendly and much liked, but was rarely seen to smile.

His expressionless face had been known to break into what could be described as a sort of smile, but only one example was stored in the communal memory. It was when he let off a monumental and extremely obnoxious fart in the mess. All those around him moved away quickly, giving him free access to a plate of food on the table. His face collapsed into a triumphant smile.

'Fatty' continued with his story. "Hitler said that the first day of the war will be the first day of the 20th century. They were the standard bearers of the 20th century to the world. It was a great responsibility. They would destroy the 19th century forever. It is the last great struggle of the 19th century and the first of the 20th. It is their great gift to the world. The world will never forget."

"What a load of bollocks," said Grzegorz. "Anyway he's got his centuries wrong. We're already well into the twentieth century."

"Anyway, it proves that our radio is in action," declared Slawomir. "And I've picked up a report that says Gydnia is on fire. Two hundred bombers are attacking and a battleship and destroyers were bombarding it."

"The trawler *'Mewa'* has beached without a crew, they were all blown overboard. Dive bombers have wrecked the Puck base. Crowds are gathering at military posts demanding arms. Officers formed a battalion of pikemen as there were no rifles for them," Slawomir added, feeling very important. There was a general groan.

"I don't think we want to know all that," said a voice

"I'm not surprised," interrupted Jan, the other telegraphist. "Last night almost every house in Gdansk had swastikas hanging from their windows."

"We've been let down by everyone," declared the Torpedo Officer Tomasz, the only bearded officer in the crew. His beard was set off by black bushy eyebrows and dark eyes. He had the habit of playing with his left earlobe when under pressure.

"We weren't allowed to mobilise. My mates in the army said that it was only 45 per cent prepared for action so we've got about 1.7 million men with little arms facing 16 panzer and motorised divisions, nearly 4,000 tanks and 4,000 aircraft. Our biggest problem is that Britain and France are our allies."

"Added to that," said Andras, "plans of the fortified zone of Silesia have been sold to the Germans by some bloody cartographer who needed the money."

"How do you know that?" asked Tomasz.

"I"ve got a friend in security who told me about it. The government kept it quiet."

Slawomir came out of the radio room again.

"They're knocking hell out of Westerplatte," he said.

* * *

Before 1914 Westerplatte was a pleasure beach. It was a sandy strip of land jutting out a kilometre into the Bay of Danzig, some 20 acres of land and small pine tress, sand dunes and pebbles. An ancient fort stood at the end. The peninsular was another piece of land given to Poland under the Treaty of Versailles as a coaling station. It was to be Poland's access to the sea. Instead the Poles had built the port of Gdynia, the biggest in the Baltic, put up in 15 years, and Westerplatte remained to all intents and purposes, unimportant.

A company of Polish solders was based there as a token of Polish control. Under the strange Versailles Agreement Danzig Germans, and they were about 90 per cent of the population, were allowed inspection privileges to see that Westerplatte remained no more than that. The French and British from time to time also sent military inspection teams to ensure that there were no fortification and therefore no provocation of the Germans. The old fort was razed to the ground.

One day a Polish major with imagination, and a pessimistic view of the future, moved to Westerplatte. He established a farm behind a new administrative building and gradually, and with great secrecy, built it into a small fortress, fully armed. By 31 August he was ready.

Now all his planning and hard work was being destroyed. Explosion followed explosion. A permanent cloud hung over the southern end of the peninsular. The *'Schleswig Holstein'* was hurling shell after shell, many falling round the only cannon in the fort. The cannon managed to land one shell on the battleship and this caused aircraft screaming in dramatic dives to come in and destroy it.

It was 4.00am on the second day of September.

To those on the submarine, which was sliding quietly through the night, it seemed that the world had been turned upside down. The atmosphere was grey with smoke and dust.

The sound was all around not receding or diminishing, but went on, madly, incredibly constant.

The lookouts kept watch for any sign of an aerial or surface attack, but apart from a lone plane, they saw nothing to cause them concern for their own safety. Then suddenly a group of aircraft seemed to be heading their way.

"Stand by. Clear the bridge, Dive, dive, dive!" ordered the Captain.

Andras and one of the signalmen were quick to react, but the order brought a feeling of terror to 17-year-old signalman Henerey. He would rather have stayed and faced the enemy, than go below into the submarine. To his dismay he had discovered, when it was too late, that he could not live in the confines of a submerged submarine. He was sure he was claustrophobic.

A fair-haired lad with a pale complexion and boyish face he had joined the Navy on an impulse. He was carried away by talk of war, a flood of patriotism and excitement. A strong urge to play his part in the struggle to come led him to the recruiting office, which without too many questions assigned him to the Navy, and sent him on a training course. He had moved quickly through a training school for signalmen and his enthusiasm and ability led to above standard marks

The chaos over mobilisation and the uncertainty of the situation had led to a number of swift decisions by the authorities and when a signal came to send ships to sea, it was found that the '*Eagle*' was undermanned and needed men. One signal indicated that a signalman was urgently needed and Henerey's top marks led to him being assigned.

* * *

All had gone well at first. When he boarded at Puck he was greeted by Andras who handed him over to Officer Cadet

Yarwin with instructions to help him find his way about the submarine. A youthful prospective officer, he was a clean cut, blonde optimist, the right man to guide Henerey.

"You been on subs before?" he asked briskly.

"No," Henerey replied nervously

"They're okay. Not much room, but you get used to it." Henerey was not so sure.

"What are you?"

"A signalman,"

"Good. So am I," Yarwin said. "Let's go below," he added, moving towards the conning tower and going down the ladder. Henerey followed uncertainly.

"This is the conning tower, obviously," Yarwin said, nodding towards the two periscopes, torpedo control and steering wheel. "Quite a lot happens here. It's where the ship is navigated. We spend a lot of time here."

"Not much room is there," Henerey commented.

"No room at all," Yarwin laughed, "you have to get used to the fact that you will never be more than two or three feet from the person next to you. Privacy doesn't exist. If you want to scratch your arse you have to make bloody sure its your own arse you're scratching otherwise it can get embarrassing," he laughed uproariously at his joke.

Henerey was horrified. He had already decided that he had made a great mistake in joining the submarine service. The sides of the conning tower were closing in on him. He could not possibly live in such a confined space and would have to ask for a transfer.

"Do many change their minds about serving on submarines?" he asked hopefully.

"What! You fed up already? You ain't seen nothing yet, as they say," Yarwin laughed happily again. "You get used to it. Anyway you have no chance of getting out now we're at sea. We don't even know where and when we will stop next. You're stuck with us. But don't worry you will get used to it. You completely forget what normal life is like and you begin to accept the cramped conditions as normal. I was a bit doubtful when I first came aboard, but now I wouldn't serve on any other sort of ship. It's my life. We're a friendly bunch, there's a good team spirit and we're proud of it. We're pretty special in submarines.

"You have to remember that a submarine is not like a surface ship, we don't have strict discipline and there's no established routine. We're a floating weapon," he went on enthusiastically. "The torpedoes are our only reason for existing, they are the only thing that matters, and sticking them into an enemy ship. The rest is by the way!"

Nothing that Yarwin was saying was helping Henerey, but his thoughts were interrupted.

"Let's get on." Yarwin moved down more. "This is the control room, the heart of the boat. Everything is run from here. That's the gyro compass, the miracle of 20th century. It's deadly accurate. Those are the hydroplane controls which control the boat when it is diving. The flooding and blowing of the ballast tanks is done from here and that," he said pointing to a small cupboard, "is the wireless cabin. I don't have to explain what happens there. And that," he added, pointing to another small cupboard, "is the galley where all the food is prepared. All cooking is done on electric heaters, but when we are at sea we don't have what you would call meals, we have eating moments when you're off duty and you get what you can. As I said, we don't have a routine we just do what has to be done when it has to be done. Exciting isn't it?"

Henerey was not finding it at all exciting. Terrifying would have been a better word, he thought.

They walked towards the stern passing other 'cupboards' which Yarwin described as the officers' and petty officers' messes. Next was the engine room with two multi-cylinder engines, two propeller shafts and the main batteries. Then came the electric motors compartment.

"We use the diesels when we are on the surface, and the electric motors when submerged. You can't use the diesels when there is no air otherwise you would suffocate everyone in seconds. They're also used to charge the electric batteries when we are on the surface, and that can be a bit tricky as you will find out." Yarwin was enjoying his role showing off his knowledge.

"And here we find the forward torpedo compartment, there's another one at the stern. There are four torpedo tubes in each. We're a bit different from some other subs because we have two twin torpedo mountings outside the hull.

"You may not have noticed it, but you have passed through the forward seamen's mess," Yarwin explained to Henerey's surprise. He looked around at the dense network of different pipes and cable, knots of valve wheels, air cylinders, depth charges, pressure gauges and indicators of all kinds. He identified what he thought were small shelves, but realized, quickly enough to avoid an embarrassing question, that they were bunks.

Yarwin followed his gaze. "Those are bunks which are shared. If you put the upper one alongside the lower one you can make a solid block. If you cover it with oil cloth you've got a comfortable couch or sofa. But you can only do this in harbour because at sea the bunks are always in use by those off duty. They have the advantage that you can have breakfast in bed simply by sticking an arm out and grabbing anything that's on the table."

He nodded towards the cupboards. "Those are small lockers for personal stuff. Not big, but big enough "cause we don't have many personal possessions."

"Where do we store things?" Henerey asked, slipping into a deeper haze every minute.

"Anywhere you can. Any gaps between machinery and

equipment, round the torpedoes, anywhere there is a space. There's a cold store below, but it doesn't hold much. There is a fresh water and a distilled water tank for the batteries, below."

"Where do we wash and shower?"

"We don't. Water is very precious and only for drinking. We have a wipe down with sea water every three or four days if we're lucky. You soon begin to realise that no-one washes."

"What sort of food do we get?"

"Potatoes, bread which is specially wrapped to last some two weeks - it is part baked ashore and after that in the galley. Other vegetables, vast amounts of tinned food, fresh water and a few cigarettes though all crammed into any available space, between instruments, machinery and equipment and between stored torpedoes - anywhere there is space. We also have ship's biscuits called hard tack, but they get a bit lively with maggots after a while. Oh, yes, you better know about lavatories."

"Do we have them?" Henerey asked with a sarcasm completely missed by Yarwin.

"Yes, but they are different. They are always beneath the sea while those on surface ships are above the water. There's a pan which can be flooded with sea water and a valve opening through the hull so that the contents can be blown out by compressed air. But it can't be used below 100 feet because of sea pressure so that's when any empty cans or containers come in useful."

"Can we smoke?"

"Only on the surface, but sometimes in the engine room. But smoking below is not much use because after a while you can't strike a match, or draw on a cigarette because there's not enough oxygen. Okay, you happy?"

"Not a word I would use," said Henerey, quite sure that he would never be happy. Nevertheless, he had a strong feeling that he was proud to be a submariner,

TWO

The Captain had taken the submarine down to 25 metres and turned sharply to port to avoid any bombs or depth charges that might have been dropped by the oncoming aircraft. The atmosphere was strained, almost to breaking point, the crew silent as they waited for their first attack not knowing what it would be like. They were locked in a steel box deep in water under pressure. What would the first explosion be like? What would be its effect? It was impossible to imagine something that was unlike anything they had experienced before.

But nothing happened. Unexpectedly, instead of enabling them to relax, the lack of action had the opposite effect, anxiety grew and anticipation became intense. It seemed to increase the chances that something would happen in the end. But after five or so minutes, by which time they thought it should all be over, there was a cautious change of mood, a feeling of anti climax which eventually resulting in a buzz of conversation.

"Silence in the boat," the Captain ordered sharply." It is not over yet." But it was.

There was nothing to alarm anyone.

"Must have had other plans," observed Andras, "or else they did not see us." The Captain nodded. It was still a question of 'what next?' A look from his First Lieutenant asked the unspoken question.

For the Captain the future seemed like a visit to a theatre where the stage was empty, there was no list of characters, no scenery, no programme, no idea of what was going to happen or how long it would last. It had the additional horror of not being sure whether you would be able to go home safely afterwards. What actually faced him was the Baltic Sea, 370,000 square kilometres of water, full of unknown difficulties, mines, enemy ships and aircraft, storms, raging tides, and dangerous shallow waters, a vast proportion of which were not really deep enough for a submarine. And the bottom line was the knowledge, which gripped the nerves in the pit of his stomach, that it was his responsibility, and his alone. He sighed deeply, hoping no-one would notice.

"We'd better start doing what we were sent here to do, look for Germans and sink them. We'll go across the Bay first to check on the situation. Get the engineer to report on our fuel reserves, and ask the Bosun to report on food supplies and that sort of thing.

Then we can decide what we can do."

But any discussion on future plans was pre-empted by the sudden arrival of the telegraphist.

"Signal Sir," he reported, "Trouble."

The Captain glanced at the paper thrust towards him. "*I have been attacked by anti-submarine boats and require immediate assistance at 54 degrees 50 minutes North and 19 degrees 30 minutes East.*" It was without signature.

"Who could it be?" asked Andras. "All the subs are out in the Bay minelaying."

The other four submarines, *'Vulture'*, *'Wild Cat'*, *'Lynx'* and *'Wolf'* had all left Gdynia before *'Eagle'*. They knew two had earlier been sent to try and reach Britain. The Captain and Andras moved towards the chart table and plotted the reported position on the chart. They checked their own position.

"She's about 80 kilometres away," Andras suggested.

"Set course and full speed," the Captain replied. "And tell the engine room what it is for, that will concentrate their minds."

Approaching the search area the Captain brought the *'Eagle'* up to periscope depth and quickly searched around the horizon.

"Nothing in sight," he reported, "not even Germans."

For three hours, assisted by Andrzej the Lieutenant of Submarine in charge of day-to-day running of the boat, they vainly carried out a painstaking search. There was no sign of their damaged colleague. Nothing.

Suddenly the Captain snapped "Down periscope dive, dive, dive, hard a-starboard. aircraft coming."

The submarine dipped dramatically and turned sharply making those who were standing lurch and grab the nearest piece of equipment.

Without warning a gigantic fist smashed into the side of the submarine throwing it sideways, and before the crew had recovered, another explosion threw them in the other direction. More depth charges, shattered glass, extinguished main lighting, and caused gushing leaks from sprung valves. Emergency lighting was switched on giving the scene a dark red glow. The noise was ear shattering, the continuous vibrations nerve-racking.

For Henerey and his shipmates this was much worse than even the most pessimistic had expected. But there was no sign of panic. Any such thoughts were immediately calmed by the imperturbability of the Captain who gave his orders in the same matter-of-fact tone that he always used. If he wasn't panicking, why the hell should they, was the general reaction.

"Take her down to 50 metres," he ordered. Again the submarine dipped dramatically.

"What's the bottom here?" he asked Piotr.

"Some 75 metres or thereabouts."

"We'll go down and wait."

The silence, which was total when the *'Eagle'* had settled on the bottom, was an unwelcome opportunity for the sailors of all ranks, despite their apprehension, to sink back into their own thoughts, into the sadness of their situation and that of their loved ones.

Seaman Guayne's deepest concern was not with his family. His mother and father had been killed in an accident when he was eight, and he had been brought up by his maternal grandparents. They had subsequently died, his grandmother just before he joined the Navy, and his grandfather shortly afterwards. Guayne's main concern was for his best friend and he felt very guilty about it.

His friend was *'Chopin'*, a small cheeky Pomeranian dog with long silky ears, a pointed nose and pricked ears. The name was inspired by the fact that whenever he got excited, or yawned, he gave a musical squeak. Whether the choice of name was a compliment to the great Polish composer, or an implied criticism, was never made clear.

Guayne loved his dog, they had gone everywhere together and it had been heart-breaking when he had to leave him with a friend when he joined up, but he had no choice.

His ambition was to get back on leave and see him again. Now it might be years before he would have the chance and it was almost certain that *'Chopin'* would be dead and gone. He was sad, but he said nothing to his shipmates, they would never understand and, any way, they had much more serious concerns.

He studied his fellow crew members closely, looking upon them as the only family he had. Clearly they were all desperately worried, but they all tried to hide their fears in jokes and meaningless banter.

Seaman Waldemar's thoughts concerned the decision he

made when he volunteered to join the war, and whether it was the right one. Rough and ready and not overly concerned with his appearance, he had a well weathered face with pug nose and a mass of wavy, uncontrolled fair hair.

An unassuming country boy, and enthusiastically patriotic, when he realised that he would have to join the armed services to defend his country he decided, like many of his colleagues, that the land and air forces and even the surface Navy, would stand little chance against the German forces. The only possible way to strike a blow for his country, he thought, was in the submarine service. All his family background was in farming, but he had discovered during recruiting tests that he had a mechanical mind, so he trained to be a stoker and work on a diesel engine. He fitted in, and enjoyed it.

What he had seen in Gdansk and Gdynia confirmed the view he had held since he was a boy, that the country was the only place to live, particularly Skorcz where he came from. He went into silent reverie thinking about his home. It's September, he reflected, a time when the crops were either in or stacked in the fields, giving the countryside a golden look which, when the sun set, turned to a comfortable brown.

It was the time of family group meetings when the old men complained that things were much better when they were running things, and young people would explain that when they took over things would be much better. Trouble was, they never could explain exactly how they would do it.

The women, he reflected, worked so hard that they were old before they were 30, there was no running water or electricity, in the winter they were cold and in the spring they were hungry. He had seen people eating in restaurants in Gdansk where they had more food on the table than a peasant saw in one week. These people got water from a tap in the wall, they did not have to walk a couple of miles to the river and carry it back.

But, he thought, it was real life, living with nature and facing up to the hardships. The future, if ever the war ended, could only be worse. He feared what he would find if he ever got back.

Bulky was the word that sprang to mind when Zygmont was spoken about. Around 1.7 metres, translated into two metres - according to him - he had all the joviality usually associated with plump people. It did not worry him, for he carried his weight with enthusiasm. He had a face resembling a mud slide, most of it had slipped around his lower cheeks and chin. The mud slide analogy could be applied to his body, which had also re-assembled itself around his waist and bottom. His hair style was original, it all lay on his head where it had grown and had rarely, if ever, seen the delights of a comb or brush and looked like a disorganised haystack flattened occasionally by a sweep of the hand. His annoying habit was finishing off people's sentences before they did, or anticipating the ending, usually killing the story. He came from a family of shopkeepers. They had been running a general story in Kwidzyn on the banks of the Vistula River in Eastern Pomerania. It was the sort of shop where people went for almost everything knowing, however obscure, the chances were that it would be in stock. Now, he thought, the chances are they would have nothing.

Guayne was anxious to take control of the conversation again.

"We'll beat the buggers in the end," he told those around him. A sardonic cheer greeted his observation.

"It's true," he said with emphasis "Kill all their officers and you've won the war. The German soldier is incapable of thinking for himself, he just obeys orders, so if you kill the officers they don't know what to do. It's all over."

"You can't kill all the officers," suggested Leading Seaman Jake. "They hide behind their men, they're like all officers."

"Since when did I hide behind you?" The stentorian voice of Torpedo Office Tomasz asked.

A shamefaced Jake stuttered. "I was not talking about naval officers, Sir."

* * *

Most of the conversation had been heard by Chief Petty Officer Tadeusz, a 25-year-old cheerful man, who was known for his light, laughing manner, but who could be dictatorial when the need arose. He was a stocky extrovert who saw the best side of everything. He saw his close cropped hair, the result of self-cropping, as an indication to others that he could be tough if driven to it.

He had been watching the scene carefully, to judge reactions to the attack, and had noticed Henerey, one of the mechanics, cringing in a corner near the main bilge pump.

His eyes were closed and his hands gripped a nearby pipe so hard that the knuckles were white.

"Are you all right?" he asked kindly.

"Yes, Sir, fine," replied the seaman quietly.

"Well you don't look it. What's wrong?"

"I'm sorry Sir," said Henerey looking up through creased eyebrows, his black eyes darting and uncertain, "but I'm a bit frightened. I can't help it."

"Frightened? I'm bloody terrified," said Tadeusz, laughing gently. The shocked comment made Henerey look up properly. "You, Sir?"

"Of course, anyone who says they're not is a bloody liar or totally insane. You just have to do your best to accept the situation and hope for the best."

"That's not all," said Henerey, now determined to tell the truth and get it off his chest in the hope that steps could be taken to change things. He had no idea what those steps might be.

"I'm frightened because I think I am claustrophobic."

"Claustrophobic?" an amazed Tadeusz asked, with a glimmer of smile of disbelief on his face. "And you joined the bloody submarine service," his amazement continued. He still kept his voice low so that others would not hear what was being said.

"I didn't know until we went to sea. I was okay on the surface, even when I went below, because the hatches were open and I did not feel closed in. But when we submerged and the hatches banged shut, it was if the whole world was closing in on me. I wanted to scream, and try and get out, but the explosions stopped me. Then I realised I would never get out and I came here to try and die."

"Well there's not a lot we can do about it now and you are not allowed to die on duty, you would be put on report and punished," Tadeusz said sympathetically. "We're not going to get out for a while yet so we have to do the best we can, you have to try and take a more expansive view. Where are you from?"

"Kwidzyn, same as Zygmont although I did not know him then."

"Well that's on the Vistula isn't it, with agricultural land all around with expansive views of green fields and woods? When you feel that the world is closing in on you, all you have to do is close your eyes and imagine you are looking across the river at the spacious, beautiful scenery. Try and imagine how far into the distance you can see. Think of some landmarks you can remember. Forget the world around you and really concentrate." Tadeusz looked at the pale figure with concern, but he was also considering the implications of a weak link in the crew chain.

Henerey nodded as though he understood. "You keep saying we?" said Henerey., "who do you mean, we?"

"You are not on your own, you know. We are a team, we have to work together, we all understand how it feels on your first trip, and will try and help you with this. But what exactly are you afraid of?" he asked, and then answered his own question. "Basically people who say they are claustrophobic really mean they are frightened because they cannot see, or feel, a way out when the world is coming in on them."

Henerey nodded.

"Think about it. You know damn well that the sides of this submarine are not coming in on you while you're sitting there. If they do come in through a depth charge you won't know anything about it."

"Yes, I realise that, but it is as though I can't breathe...." Henerey tried to interrupt.

"You're breathing now. If you were on a small ship like a minesweeper or a minelayer on the surface would you feel like you do?" Henerey shook his head."But you would be living and working in a mess exactly the same size as this one on the sub. Some 12 to 15 men, living together in a space six metres long and five metres wide. It's cramped and airless and bloody uncomfortable.

"If you were attacked on one of those ships you could escape. But to where? Most likely you'd jump into the sea and drown. And what is worse, if you are on a small surface ship the enemy can see you clearly and take pot shots at you for as long as they like. You've no defence. But in a submarine the bastards have no idea where you are, they have to guess and they usually guess badly and miss. You are really very much safer down here," declared Tadeusz finally.

A huge explosion suddenly shook the submarine throwing everyone off their feet and hurling anything loose flying. Gradually they began to pick themselves and check themselves for damage.

"See, I told you. They've missed again," Tadeusz pointed out reasonably as he walked away.

Dasay, who never missed anything and was always looking

for trouble, walked up to Tadeusz and quietly asked; "Some sort of problem there?"

"What do you mean?" the Tadeusz snapped.

"I thought he was cracking. I have been watching him closely and I think he might do something stupid. His nerves are giving him trouble, he's scared to death."

"It's none of your business," Tadeusz told the leading seaman angrily. "You concentrate on your job and make sure you do not 'crack' as you say. Now leave him alone, and say nothing, or you will soon learn the real meaning of having a problem." Dasay nodded and slouched away.

For half an hour the explosions continued, although the noise and effects of the attack lessened as familiarity slightly reduced the fear. They began to feel they were safe. Then the noise stopped. The silence was complete, both inside and outside the boat. Was it all over?

The Captain, however, was well aware that nothing could be taken for granted. He knew the Germans were cunning enough to stop their attack, and wait on the surface hoping he would think they had gone, start up the engines and come up to periscope depth, where they would be waiting. He was not about to take any precipitate action.

* * *

It was more than two hours later that the Captain felt it was worthwhile taking a tentative look. There had been no sound from the surface for almost all of that time.

"Take it up to periscope depth, slowly," he ordered

To the relief of most of those on board the needle on the depth gauge slowly began to rise. Many felt that: they had been there for so long they might have sunk into the mud and stuck. It took an age, but gradually the submarine reached periscope depth.

"Up periscope," he said as he reach down to the handles so that he could look out as soon possible. He swung the periscope around the full circle of the horizon.

"Christ," he said quietly. "Down periscope."

He turned to Andras "There are dozens of them up there, including two destroyers luckily they are some distance away to the north west." Andras said nothing, but raised his eyebrows quizzically.

"We can't wait round here" came the answer, "we'll have to go east away from them.

East?" another lift of the eyebrows. "Are you sure?"

"Yes."

"That's where our minefield is," Andras pointed out hesitantly.

* * *

THREE

The Captain turned his steely blue eyes on his Number One.

"Are you quite sure?"

"Absolutely. I saw a chart at base. I've a friend in the defence section and I was talking to him, I only glanced at it, but it showed a minefield marked, two actually, but don't ask me anything about them, where they are, or their extent. I'm not even sure whether they were ours or the Germans, or both. They both lie between us and the Gulf. Trouble is that the water is bloody shallow so we might have to slide along the bottom."

"Well, we know the *'Vulture'* and the *'Lynx'* were sent out to lay mines, but we can't call them up and ask them where they did it. What do we know about minefields, especially ours, how do we drop them, in sequence to a plan or haphazardly, are they moored or just thrown overboard and left to drift? What depth do we usually give them?" the Captain asked generally.

The Officers around him looked blank.

"I once had a discussion with a minelayer Captain, Sawicki of the *'Vulture'*," said Torpedo Officer Tomasz, playing with the lobe of his left ear, a sure sign of his inner tension. "We talked about the principles of minelaying in general and their purpose. We assumed we'd be attacked by surface ships if war came, but we never discussed U-boats, so I would suggest they would be moored in the shallower waters to catch surface craft.

"That's what I would do anyway. It was rumoured that the Germans had something called a magnetic mine, mines attracted by the magnetism of the steel hull, and if that's the case we're in trouble."

"Thank you," said the Captain curtly, "I will decide whether we are in trouble."

"The question is, how many mines are there likely to be out there if we dropped them?" Andras pondered.

"We know the *'Vulture'* and *'Lynx'* were sent out to lay mines and they would carry around 20 each," said Jersey.

"But we also had mine-laying trawlers out there and they carry many more than that," Tomasz added.

"There must be at least 100 out there," offered Jersey. "Still, there's one thing. I reckon it would be better to be blown up by our own mines rather than German. They would not get any satisfaction out of it." His remark was greeted by moans, half-hearted smiles and quiet chuckles.

"It will be like a blind man crossing a narrow plank zig-zag bridge with no sides over a lake. It can not be done," said the new Gunnery Officer Mucha, defiantly.

"We will have a go through the minefield," the Captain declared matter-of-factly, ignoring the comment, "and put our faith in the Almighty. The depth here is around 30-50 metres," he added quizzically, glancing at the Number One who nodded.

"Right, go to 40 metres, steer 350 degrees. Slow ahead both, close all water-tight doors and hatches, close up diving crew." He threw an acrimonious look at Mucha. It was a silent rebuke which warned him that the Captain would be watching him closely. Mucha noticed it regretfully.

* * *

The Captain called for the Coxswain and Bosun, Stefan and Jacek

"This is where you two come into your own," he said, looking at them both directly, giving them confidence.

"Steering is not going to be easy Stefan ," you will need steady nerves, I'm sure you will handle it. Jacek, keep your eye on the men and see they stay steady, I am sure they will, but show you are interested in them."

The two men saluted.

When Stefan and Jacek first met at Primary School they immediately became friends. They were both keen on sport, they were at the same level scholastically and they spent most of their spare time down at Gdynia harbour watching the ships coming and going. They both decided they wanted to be sailors. They both went to the High School, where they retained the same intellectual level, they discovered girls and what you could do with them, if you were lucky, and they passed out at the same level. They still went down to the port regularly and they still wanted to be sailors.

Much to their families' grief they both volunteered for the Navy when their parents had hoped they would show more ambition and go into a profession which had a good social standing. They went through training together and coincidentally met girls who were to become their wives - Stefan to Ewa, Jacek to Teresa - who, to the surprise of no-one, were sisters.

There were, of course, differences. Stefan followed in his father's footsteps and grew to be two metres tall; Jacek tried hard to emulate this, but could only manage 1.7 metres. Stefan was bony, slim-hipped with brown eyes and brown hair; Jacek was muscular, barrel-chested, fair haired with green/brown eyes. Stefan was stubborn and impatient, while Jacek was laid back and open to persuasion.

Both men received promotion at the same time and became Petty Officers. When the call went out for volunteers for the submarine service there was no discussion, they both volunteered.

The Captain of the *'Eagle'* had looked at them with interest when they came aboard.

"I see you know each other," he said, looking at the records.

"For about 15 years, Sir," said Stefan

"And we've been together ever since we met," Jacek added. "That is why we wanted to join the *'Eagle'* at the same time. We work well together, Sir."

"It could be useful," said the Captain. "I need two senior Petty Officers, one as Coxswain and the other as Bosun. They need to work together to help produce an efficient ship. Who would like to do what?"

Stefan smiled: "I think I should take over as Coxswain, Sir, as I can steer a ship, Jacek might take you anywhere. He would be better as Bosun because he works well with men and understands the equipment." Jacek nodded his agreement.

Despite the façade of two boys, close as brothers, the alliance between the two was not as cast iron as appearances led their colleagues to believe. Jacek, for one, was getting tired of a relationship he described to himself as "Siamese twins" joined together by the conviction of outsiders. The general view that they were a pair was becoming tiresome.

He was an individual and wanted to be seen as such; Stefan too secretly felt that their apparent inseparability was affecting his promotion prospects.

"You have chosen the tricky job," the Captain smiled, "because the waters of the Baltic are shallow and treacherous. The men are pretty well behaved and all the equipment works, as far as I know. Welcome to the ships' company gentlemen."

Stefan had no idea exactly how difficult his job would turn out to be.

* * *

Nervous tension is infectious and it swept through the submarine with the speed of a measles epidemic in a primary school. Henerey was riveted to his valve controls as if he was an integral part of the steel component. His concentrated stare at the valve dial had all the intensity of a laser beam.

Tadeusz was the odd one out, walking around with a calm and confident attitude.

"Don't worry lads if you are conscious you are still alive. Just keep breathing, it's good for you," he said amicably. A few faces relaxed into weak smiles.

Sliding through the sea encased in a steel chamber, in an unknown environment, with no idea where you are going and only a demoralising concept of what is ahead, knowing that in a split second life would be terminated, was not the most encouraging environment in which to exist. Its problems, the future, the past, the present – could all be expunged in a flash.

It was all a matter of luck. Or was it up to God? But why should God be merciful to the crew of the *'Eagle'* when their loved ones are being subjected to unknown horrors? Why should God listen to you now that you are in trouble when you haven't given him a thought for years? Is my life worth saving? What have I done to make it so? A whole cluster of past sins and errors passed through the minds of the petrified crew. Most of them concluded hopefully that whatever they had done, or bad thoughts they had had, none of them deserved a death sentence. But then, close relations like their mothers, fathers, sisters and brothers had done nothing to deserve what they may well be going through in the hands of the Germans.

Jersey, the engineering officer, closely watching how his machinery was behaving, thought of his father who, he had been told just before the *'Eagle'* sailed, was close to death after a long illness. He was well out of it. At least his death was natural and he had completed his life even though, at 55 years, he was comparatively young. But his sister Krystyna, what of her? At 24 years her life had not really started and she was a gentle, innocent young woman. What would happen to her? And his wife Magda?

If she was not killed by bombs, shells or bullets, Jersey told himself, she would comply willingly with any orders, rules or regulations imposed on her simply to retain a peaceful life. He loved her dearly, but he had no idealistic misconception of how she would react. Unhappily he knew that she would do whatever was required. Whatever.

* * *

Progress continued steadily for a while when, without warning, a grating sound like a metal crate being dragged over gravel turned the sultry atmosphere in the submarine to ice. It sent a shudder of recognition through Guayne.

"It sounds like a dog scratching to get in," he said in a trembling voice.

"Well let the bugger in," snapped the uncaring Dasay. "It's not a bloody dog its a bloody mine cable, you twit."

"My dog always knocked on the door once when he wanted to come it. He was very good about that," Guayne persisted

"Shut up about your bloody dog. Dogs don't knock on doors, "Dasay persisted. "I tell you, it's a bloody mine."

The fact that it was almost certainly a mine cable certainly concentrated the mind. Somehow, only feet away, or perhaps inches, was a mine full of explosives which could blow them into eternity.

Silence.

Apprehension intensified to an agonising level.

The sword of Damocles was hanging over their heads and could be dropped at any moment. Another scratch. Most of the crew were now awash with sweat, others increasingly found that their bladders were becoming uncontrollable. Some were trying to build a mental picture of the outside of the hull of the submarine, trying to remember whether there was any protruding part which could snag the cable and drag the mine onto them. Dasay's announcement had certainly concentrated the mind.

Suddenly the stillness was unexpectedly shattered.

"How do you know when you are dead?" a quiet voice suddenly asked. It was Jake, a leading seaman, a thoughtful member of the crew and a man with a reputation as a gambler. Of medium height, with a cheerful open face, he was a friend to all, and a natural instigator of conversation and discussion

"What the hell are you talking about?" Dasay asked, annoyed that someone was attempting to take over the conversation.

In the forward torpedo compartment where 18 men were incarcerated, the atmosphere was like an oven. Condensation dripped from pipes, overhead cables and machinery, accentuating the dampness of the sweating occupants. Eyes were glued to the bow of the submarine, a few feet away from them, and they envisaged it slowly approaching a moored mine. They would be the first to go. But only by a matter of seconds.

"How do you know that you are dead?" Jake repeated with emphasis. "Better still, do you actually know you are dead and you're not going to see anyone you know again?"

"What are you going on about?" An angrier Dasay , his own nerves at breaking point, was nearing loss of control.

"I would not mind seeing some of the girls I have known," offered 19-year-old, Hreinski, who was well known for his sexual enthusiasm and single minded approach to the subject. His pale face, spotty skin and his lifeless eyes were a clear indication of his erstwhile life style. The idea that he might have higher, or even different, concerns was a novelty.

"It's a simple question. One minute you are alive, the next minute you are dead. Do you suddenly wake up somewhere else, in an other world, and think 'bugger me I am dead'?" Jake went on.

"What do you think Lukasz?"

Lukasz, was a leading seaman who, at 27 years, was looked upon as one of the senior members of the lower ranks. Before talk of imminent war changed a million or more lives, he had planned to join the church and become a priest. His ambition was most likely inspired by the influence of his birthplace, Wejherowo, once known as the centre of religious tolerance in Poland. Over the years however, during which Protestantism became unpopular, it had become a strong centre of Catholicism. His parents were devout Catholics, attending almost every service on offer, and used the power of parental persuasion to make him go with them. He started with the initial enthusiasm of his parents, but had then begun to ask questions, a practice his parents would never have contemplated. The outbreak of war and all it meant in disaster and death didn't help. His thoughts were suddenly interrupted when he realised a question was being aimed at him.

"You planned to be a priest?" Jake asked.

"I thought about it, but it's all irrelevant now."

"What do you mean?" asked Jake. Lukasz was not surprised by the question, he had had his leg pulled many times in the past whenever questions concerning religion had arisen. "Ask the Pope" was a common comment when questions arose.

"It depends on what you believe," said Lukasz, "If you think there is an after-life......"

"You will expect someone to be there to meet you and show you the ropes. They would tell you that were dead," interrupted Zygmont logically.

"Depends whether you believe in heaven and hell," said

another voice from the depths of the compartment, hidden from the leading conversationalists by a small group of bodies.

"We are in hell at the moment," muttered another voice. "Anywhere else would be heaven." There was an outbreak of light laughter, but most of those present took the conversation seriously.

"I have an interesting theory about this," Officer Cadet Marek joined in. "I reckon that when you die you go up and report to St. Peter. He looks at your record on Earth and if he thinks it's a good one he lets you go on into Heaven. But if he thinks it's pretty ropey he tells you your record is not good enough and sends you back to give you another chance."

"In other words he tells you to go to hell." Marek grinned proudly, happy with his revolutionary theory.

"That means that as time passes all the good people will be in Heaven, and all the bad guys on the Earth, so that eventually the Earth will be populated only by the rotten bastards. Should be fun," offered Dayas joyously. "That means that most of us are going to be around for a long time."

"What a boring prospect, a world full of only good people," offered Eryk. "Bloody ghastly."

The others looked at each other in baffled silence

"What about you Gregorsz?"

"Why me?"

"Well you come from the same town as Lukasz. Are you religious?"

"You do not have to be religious just because you come from Wejherowo," Gregorsz replied disparagingly. "I was going to study law, but according to my father you can't believe in God and be a lawyer at the same time. I wanted a steady job with regular hours and a wife and children to go home to."

"So you joined the bloody Navy?"

"Very funny. It was obvious I had to join up and fight. The

Navy seemed the most acceptable. I heard that officialdom and discipline are less restrictive in the submarine service." Grezgorz was a relaxed town boy, rough and ready, who joined the Navy because he thought it was the safest of the three services. "I had no desire to go marching for bloody miles and get shot at by some unfriendly sod with a gun, nor did I have any intention of getting into a box and flying in the air. If God had wanted us to fly he would have given us bloody wings. In the Navy you can swim to safety or drown and I'm told drowning is quite a pleasant experience."

"Who do you know who has drowned?" asked a sceptical Jake.

"It's an accepted fact," replied Dasay sharply.

"I am serious about death," Jake insisted heatedly, trying to get back control of the conversation. "I cannot imagine not being here."

"If you were not here you would not be able to imagine it." Dasay informed him curtly.

"Think about it. If the next depth charge blows us all to Kingdom come, we're gone. That's the end of it. What's next?"

A new voice, 28-years-old seaman Waldemar, joined the conversation which was making a serious contribution to relieving the tension.

"You ought to be grateful it's so quick If you're in the army or air force and get shot you could be on your own, injured for life, hobbling about, blind or deaf. If you're one of us you've no such problem. We all go together."

"You might end up in the next world crippled, blind or deaf, and that would be forever," suggested a sceptical Gzregorz.

"Too deep for me," said Lukasz. "As far as I am concerned that's it. No problem."

"Yes," insisted Jake, "but do you know that's it. It's no bloody good if you don't actually know it's all over."

"I bet you a week's pay we won't be hit," said Jake, getting back into character and lowering the tone. A seaman from Ostroda in East Prussia, a former German province, he was unsure where his family originated. His grand parents had been among the many people who had been moved to the area from all parts of Poland, so the population was a mixture of Germans and Poles. But he was in no doubt that he was Polish and proud of it.

He had an ambivalent approach to the war. On the one hand he was naturally concerned for his family, on the other hand his emotion was one of relief for, as a habitual gambler, he had left many debts behind when the *'Eagle'* sailed. These would not now have to be settled in the short term, and it was unlikely that they would ever have to be.

His last venture had been to bet all those who were interested, that the German would not invade Poland in 1939. Everyone around him at the time had been the worse for drink, and had been unable to work out that if he lost the bet his ship would have sailed long before pay out time came. If he won the bet he would have been around to pick up his winnings.

"Bloody typical," snapped Hreinski, "if we are hit you won't have to pay up. If we get away with it we will all have to pay."

"But you will feel better, being alive to pay," laughed Jake.

"You really are a stupid sod," announced Dasay, "it does not matter a bugger if we live or die."

Silence.

There was no desire among those present to start an argument with Dasay, a pleasant enough man, but one who could take exception to any proposal or suggestion. A punchy little man he was extremely fit and bubbling with energy like a fully trained boxer with no-one to fight. There was never a chance that he would actually punch anybody, but the energy he put into an argument was disconcerting.

"There are people who believe that in the next world you meet all the people you knew when they were alive on earth," declared Lukasz.

"Jesus Christ, I hope not," said Dasay, "if I see my father again I will kill him."

"He is already dead," Jake pointed out.

"Well, I will do something," he declared impatiently, "after the way he treated me when I was a lad."

Silence again as thoughts of who they might meet in the next world took over The overriding thought was that they had no idea what had happened to the families and friends they had left behind when the war started. And they might never know.

It suddenly had a much more serious and heart-breaking meaning.

The submarine crept on. Tension slackened slightly.

* * *

In the control room another crisis had developed. The Captain was clearly unwell and it had nothing to do with their distressing situation. He was, in fact, desperately ill. Before they had entered the minefield he had spent a considerable amount of time in his cabin, visited every now and then by his First Lieutenant He had now been in the control room for several hours, grey and sombre and obviously in pain. But, as he told his officers, it was something about which he did not wish to speak. He could manage and all they had to worry about was obeying orders and getting *'Eagle'* through the minefield.

The actual control of the submarine was now in the hands of Andras who worked closely with Engineer Jersey and the Senior Lieutenant Piotr. Andras was concentrating his mind on what he had seen on the chart at base, all he could recall were two shaded areas; there was no indication of how the mines had been laid, or any pattern, or even how many mines had been planted.

"There's not a lot we can do, but go straight ahead at slow speed and hope for the best. If we try altering course, making wild guesses, we could be going straight into trouble. Where should we alter course, when and why? We really have no choice at all," Andras told his colleagues. They nodded slowly in agreement.

Another half hour passed in almost complete silence and very little movement The danger of going through the minefields was translated into the illogical feeling that if they moved they might nudge the submarine into a passing mine.

Another grating sound, this time like the drawing of chalk on a blackboard, another mine cable, the return of almost unacceptable tension.

* * *

Torpedo Officer Tomasz went up to the chart table to check the situation. The gunnery Petty Office Marcin was already there. They did not speak. In fact, they rarely even acknowledged each other's presence. It had been noted by almost every member of the crew that something was wrong between them.

Marcin was a tough looking guy with a strong, square face and a chin that looked like a lump of granite. His large ears stuck out slightly causing some unwise crew members to use the nickname "Jumbo" behind his back. Anyone ill-informed enough to do so within his hearing did well to immediately adopt a defensive stance. Despite his appearance he was, in fact, a softie. As a boy he had been promising young boxer, but he had given it up because he did not like gaining pleasure out of hurting his opponent. The fact that it was he who could have been hurt never seemed to occur to him, and it rarely happened. But his mind was now in constant turmoil. It involved a vivid memory of the past which, despite his efforts, continually crowded in upon him.

It involved his torpedo officer. Tomasz had been going out with a girl, Alina, for several years, they had become engaged much to the family's delight and were making marriage plans.

Then Marcin had been invited to a party at the home of a friend of a friend and had met a girl called Alina. The sexual chemistry was immediate. There was mutual attraction. He pursued her and she was impressed because he cut a dashing figure as a man of action, a man in charge of himself. Tomasz gradually faded into the background of the girl's mind. The wedding arrangements had almost been finalised when she finally decided to abandon Tomasz and run off with Marcin. She failed to say anything to Tomasz, but he had a suspicion that all was not well.

He had been shattered, kicking himself that he had allowed his devotion to the Navy to blind him to his domestic life and his responsibilities. When he finally met up with Marcin he lost all self-control, launching himself at him and starting a vicious fight. Tomasz lost both the fight and the girl.

When Tomasz had been assigned to the *'Eagle',* only days before it sailed, he was appalled to recognise that a senior member of the gunnery team, was Marcin, the man responsible for breaking up his impending marriage.

As the Captain greeted him and turned towards Marcin to introduce him, both men stood shocked and speechless, looking at each other.

For Tomasz the events of the past months, images of his lovely wife-to-be, memories of how he learned the truth, the humiliation of how he felt, all passed before him in a confused flash. For Marcin it was a feeling of dread that overcame him. Here he was, on a warship with a war about to start, with the strict discipline of the Navy imbibed in him, facing a superior officer whose fiancée he had stolen, who he had beaten in a fight, and whose life he could have destroyed.

The two men stared at each other without expression.

"I see you know each other," said the Captain. It was not a question. It was a statement which recognised that something was wrong and that it was serious. Both men nodded, still holding each other with their eyes.

"Clearly something has happened in the past which I do not wish to know about," the Captain said impatiently. "I will just say this. Any animosity you feel towards each other must immediately be forgotten. We will soon be at war. Our only purpose is to obey orders and fight the enemy. We will become an efficient fighting machine in which everyone, I repeat everyone, will play their part. Nothing, absolutely nothing, must be allowed to interfere with that. Do you both hear me?" Tomasz and Marcin snapped to attention and replied, "Yes, Sir."

Both men had accepted the order as they knew they had no choice, but had kept well away from each other. The lack of communication and the animosity was noticed by other members of the crew, and there was intense speculation, but no-one dared ask what the problem was.

Warrant Officer Kazik, a big man who carried his air of authority with ease, was one who noticed the antagonism. He was particularly interested because it concerned a petty officer and a commissioned officer. Kazik was a professional sailor who lived by the book. He had, however, learned to temper his demands for discipline in the more relaxed, but infinitely more dangerous, life on a submarine. He could come down hard if required, but this was rarely called upon on the *'Eagle'*.

Only once had he had to use his authority to the full. It was when Dasay was being riled by Jake. Dasay had turned nasty during an argument with Hreinski and Jake had interfered by telling Hreinski to "have patience with Dasay because I think it's his time of the month."

"What the hell do you mean by that?" Dasay had snapped.

"Nothing. It was a remark of sympathy. I know it can be a very difficult time," Jake had added, making matters worse. Dasay had taken an almighty swipe at Jake who, fortunately, had side-stepped just in time. Kazik had seen what happened and as it was a case of a seaman attacking a leading seamen, and therefore of higher rank, Dasay had to be punished. He had been put on cleaning lavatories duties, both those of the officers and seamen on the submarine, for a week. Dasay had done this many times as a matter of routine, but to have to do it as a punishment was unacceptable demeaning.

Another hour passed on their dangerous journey without any further alarms and it gradually seemed that they were in the clear.

"We should be through by now," Andras suggested to the suffering Captain. "What do you think about surfacing and getting some fresh air?"

The Captain turned to him, his face drawn and grey. "Yes, Andras, take her up."

* * *

The order from the Captain to surface sent a new range of emotions and tensions through the crew. The instant reaction was the excitement and relief of breathing air unpolluted by sweat, rotting food, damp clothes and body odours. But it was countered by the thought of what might be waiting them on the surface, enemy ships or, still worse, mines.

The bow of the submarine rose and began its dignified journey to the surface. It had been under attack, experienced a prolonged period at a comparatively great depth, found its way through a minefield and now brought the crew safely towards the surface.

'Eagle' was therefore already a submarine of some

distinction. Built in Holland and funded by public subscription, it was commissioned into the Polish Navy in February 1939. The original design advanced for the proposed submarine, was far bigger than any other submarine in the fleets of the Baltic nations. What was required by the forward-thinking Poles of that time was a larger submarine to ensure seaworthiness and habitability in the rough waters of the Baltic. It also had to be able to carry and provide provisions for at least 30 days. In the course of subsequent events the proposals could be seen as prophetic and contributed significantly to what happened.

What they got was a submarine of some 117,000 tons on the surface, 84 metres long and with a beam of 6.57 metres and a draught of 4.17m. It could dive to a depth of 80 metres and sail over 1,000 kilometres at 10 knots on the surface and 160 kilometres submerged.

She had a crew of six officers, 18 Petty Officers including four Officer Cadets, and 30 seamen.

In normal circumstances submarine crews were carefully selected to ensure as far as possible that those chosen were compatible. The aim was to produce a group of men who were reliable, gregarious, confident, adaptable, resourceful, calm and steady and, of course, skilled in their individual fields. As events had occurred so quickly most of the last minute vacancies on the *Eagle* had to be filled on an availability basis. A cynic in the crew expressed the view that if the Medical Officer looked in one ear and could not see out through the other you were in.

Happily most members of the crew which sailed from the Puck base in Gdynia Bay on 1 September were well balanced and fitted the criteria and, encouraged by the tragic events, they had quickly formed a determined team.

The only major bone of contention was between Tomasz and Marcin, but they were professional enough not to let their personal problems interfere with their professional roles.

* * *

One partnership that played an important role in the life of the submarine by helping to lighten the tension, enlivening and inspiring the crew was that of Officer Cadets Eryk and Marek, each 18 years old, who were both alike and different. Both took their position seriously, but while Eryk was light hearted Marek took a more serious approach laced with humour on occasions.

When asked why he was an Officer Cadet, Marek would explain that he wanted to be a professional officer and to do this he had to start as a learner, finding our how the lower ranks lived, what they worried about, and how they performed their duties. Then he would remind the questioners that an awful lot is expected of an officer. They had to know the basics of seamanship, navigation and ship management, but also have a basic knowledge of gunnery, torpedoes, mine handling, electric systems, mathematics, visual signalling wireless and other subjects. All this knowledge helped to make a professional officer, he concluded. Most people ended up wishing they had never asked.

Their characters were almost a reflection of their home towns. Eryk. like Yarwin, was born and lived in Sopot. Marek came from Tczew on the lower Vistula some 35km from Gdansk. Its only claim to fame, apart from its rich farmland, was that it was one of the bases of the Teutonic Order of Knights when fighting heathens and colonising landsin the 1200s, on behalf of the Duke of Mazowiecki. He had a much more serious attitude.

Known by most members of the crew, and the officers, unimaginatively as the 'Terrible Twins', they each had a disconcerting habit, although they expressed it in a different way. While Eryk's lively blue eyes would be darting over the shoulder of the person he was talking to, ensuring that he missed nothing. Marek's steady brown eyes would look directly into those of the person he was addressing. To many people this was very disconcerting, making them feel uncomfortable, not wishing to take part in a staring contest. Marek's view was that in this way he could tell whether the person he was talking to was genuine. There was much discussion among the crew, out of ear-shot, about what happened when they actually talked to each other.

While Marek had received a good education, thanks to his father's insistence, and his own determination to do well, Eryk had proved to be a problem to any schoolmaster who had tried in vain to put the laws of physics, mathematics and science in his head. He described himself in educational terms as 'pretty average' on the grounds that no-one would disagree with him. But he now professed that the subjects in which he had shown no interest were now important to him.

Another major difference of opinion was in their attitude to foreigners. Eryk hated the Germans with a vengeance and in view of what was happening now, with good reason. Marek placed the Russians at the top of his hate list. They had, he would explain, been a destructive influence on Poland throughout history.

Their differences came to an end when the subject turned to girls, dancing, food and chess. They both thought they were good players in the courting and dancing game and, at chess, but, in fact, they were only moderate at best.

Both spent as much time as they could in or around the control room, the heart of the submarine. They both held the view that to learn the most you have to be where the action is - the heart of the ship from where all manoeuvres for diving and surfacing the submarine are directed. The gyro compass is there, as is the operations equipment for the hydroplane which govern diving, submerging and surfacing in conjunction with the blowing and flooding of the main ballast tanks, and the pumps which control the trim, general balance and stability of the boat. They both agreed it was the only place to be.

* * *

The slow progress of the boat towards the surface was accompanied by an upsurge of relief among the men who had been confined in discomfort and fear for many hours. The fact that the boat was rising slowly was accentuated by the fact that it began to come under the influence of the movement of the sea. This was confirmed by the hissing of compressed air displacing the water from the ballast tank, and the sound of the lapping of the waves as they began to hit the sides of the hull, When the conning tower broke the surface the hatch was flung open causing a welcome rush of fresh air.

The diesel engines were started up and the accompanying noise broke the silence, and a stream of air sucked in the by the engines produced a strong enlivening gust.

In normal circumstances the Captain, the Officer of the Watch and two signalmen as lookouts would leap on to the bridge

The lookouts were the first into the fresh air. It was clear that the Captain was unable to climb the ladder up to the bridge. He could not put his leg on the ladder and exert pressure on his stomach. Each time he tried, his grimace tore the heart strings of those watching. Without a word he nodded to the Officer of the Watch, Lieutenant. Mucha, who, followed by the two signalmen, was sent up as look outs.

The Captain stood at the bottom and looked appealingly at the First Lieutenant who read his mind accurately. He turned to the Torpedo Officer who was standing by. "We will have to help him. Go up first and take his hand. I will help him from behind."

It was a pitiful sight. A proud and dignified officer clearly required help to enable him to get onto his bridge and carry out his duties. All those nearby not involved looked away and concentrated on something else as the Torpedo Officer climbed up, went on his knees and took the Captain's hand, while the First Lieutenant put his shoulder under the Captain's bottom and slowly eased him up. What would normally have taken a matter of seconds became one of minutes before the Captain was able to take up his position on the bridge. The Officer of the Watch and the lookouts had already ensured that no danger was imminent.

The Captain had planned on his next action while the submarine was still submerged and gave orders to take the 'Eagle' out into the Gulf of Danzig at half speed. Everyone on the bridge, and those below, relaxed as breathable air gushed through the submarine.

After ten minutes the First Lieutenant asked for permission to leave the bridge and went below to talk to Jersey and Tomasz.

"We have got a bit of a problem," the First Lieutenant said to his two colleagues. "The Captain's health is clearly deteriorating, something has to be done." They nodded uncomfortably, understanding the problem.

"Where is the Medical Orderly?" Andras asked.

"Here, Sir," reported Officer Cadet Kacek. It was the moment he had dreaded. With no medical knowledge he was the Medical Orderly, but through no fault of his own. The post had been ignored when, in the chaos of the hours before the war, the boat's complement had been decided. When it was realised that someone with medical knowledge would be useful, the Captain had made enquiries which ended up with Kacek.

"Your father is a doctor?" he had asked Kacek.

"Yes, Sir." Kacek replied wondering what his father's

profession had to do with anything. He and his father were not close and had rarely discussed anything of importance.

"Do you know anything about it?"

"No, Sir, nothing. I never took any interest in what he was doing because I have no interest in, or intention of, being a doctor," Kacek replied hopefully.

"Tough luck," the Captain said, smiling. "We need a Medical Officer and for the purposes of this voyage you are it. You remain a Cadet, I'll call you the Medical Orderly," he added quickly, in case Kacek saw it also as a promotion. "You must have picked up something listening to your father. We've got some books somewhere, look through them, check what equipment and medicine we've got. You start now," he had added dismissively.

Kacek had had to deal with a few cuts and bruises, given out a few pills for diarrhoea and colds, but nothing serious. He had read the medical journals from cover to cover. He did not know what menstruation was, but he was sure that if any member of the crew ever suffered from it he knew that two aspirins would probably sort it out. Haemorrhoids, he decided, he would have nothing to do with. Now, however, it was serious.

Andras looked at him.

"You recently examined the Captain, what did you say to him?"

"I said I was not sure what was wrong, but I would study the books."

"And what conclusion did you come to?"

"I honestly do not know Sir, but if I had to make an informed guess……."

"You do," Andras interrupted.

"I would say it looks a lot like typhus. He has had severe headaches, he has certainly got a fever and says he is feeling very weak. I noticed this morning when I was examining him that he has also got a rash of some sort under his armpits, according to the book that clinches it."

"How serious is it?"

"It could be very serious. Typhus killed several million people during the First World War and, as far as I know, we have nothing we could treat it with."

"Nothing at all?"

"No, Sir, we have only basic medical requirements, bandages, plasters, aspirins, creams for burns, things like that."

"Thank you." said Andras dismissively ."You have been very helpful."

Kacek walked away his stomach churning. My God! I hope I am right, he thought to himself.

* * *

After about half an hour, and with solicitous help from those around, the Captain left the bridge and returned to his cabin. Henryk smiled wanly when Andras came to see him:

"Doesn't look good does it?"

"No, Sir. I have just been talking to Kacek who examined you recently." The Captain nodded. "Although he can not be one hundred per cent certain, after looking at all the books he thinks you may have typhus. It could be quite serious."

"I must say, it feels bloody serious," said the Captain feelingly.

"Well, Sir," said the First Lieutenant hesitatingly, "it is clear that physically life is going to be very difficult for you. I believe it would be unfair to ask you to command the ship in the normal way. It's largely a matter of mobility. If, for example, you were on the bridge when we had to make an emergency dive it would be a question of saving you or the submarine. You will be the first to agree that we would have to choose the submarine. I, for one, would not like to be part of having to make that choice."

"I'm sure you would make the right one," said the Captain, smiling.

"What I suggest is that I take over all your physical duties as far as possible. You stay below unless you begin to feel stronger. I will report to you regularly, of course, and if a serious situation arises. But we have to get some treatment for you as soon as possible."

"What do you want to do, have me put down?" the Captain laughed.

"It's a thought, but too messy," replied Andras, grinning. "I think we will keep you alive for the time being. But we should be figuring out a way of getting you to a hospital."

The Captain looked at the First Lieutenant seriously: "Do you think Kacek is right?"

"He is a reliable lad," Andras replied solemnly. "He takes it all very seriously. He has studied the various medical books we have on board and says, you have all the symptoms."

The Captain frowned. "Bad as that?" he said.

"Of course we can't be sure, but I think if we plan for the worst we can't go wrong. Getting you some treatment is the priority."

* * *

At that moment the Engineering Officer Jersey came in looking serious, and joined the group.

"We've got a problem," he said.

Christ! Not another one, thought Andras.

Jersey glanced towards the Captain his mind quickly taking in the irony of the situation. His own father was dying and he had had to abandon him when the *'Eagle'* sailed. Now he was faced with another person, who he held in the highest esteem, looking as though he was not going to last long.

Jersey had been at the base making last minute

arrangements about his engines and spare parts, checking that all was well, when he had been called to the telephone. It was his sister to tell him that according to the doctor his father had not got long to live and had asked to see him. Jersey was overwhelmed to find himself in such an impossible position. War was about to start, his ship had been ordered to sail, and his dying father wished to see him. Which, he asked himself, came first, his love for his father and his last request, or his duty to his country at a time of conflict.

There was not really a choice, there was nothing he could do even if he went home to his father except say 'goodbye' If he chose to abandon his ship at this critical time and went to see his father he would not be able to live with the fact that he had deserted his shipmates when they needed him. He could do nothing for his father, but he was vital to his submarine's operation and his shipmates.

He had in his charge two powerful multi-cylinder diesel engines which drove the two main propeller shafts and charged the main batteries. He also had two electric motors which provided the motive power for the ship when submerged; air compressors which were used to blow the main ballast tanks when the submarine surfaced and provided air for the torpedoes, and for blowing various internal trimming and domestic tanks; and equipment for vaporizing and atomizing the liquid fuel. It was these latter pieces of equipment which had brought him rushing to report to the Captain.

"It's the compressor," explained, "it is badly cracked. And the evaporator is broken. I think as a result of that last depth charge attack."

"Can they be repaired?" asked the Captain.

"No, Sir, not while we are at sea. We need a dockyard with the right equipment. It wouldn't take long, but we cannot do it at sea."

"What will happen if we don't get them repaired?"

"The efficiency of the submarine will be seriously diminished and we will eventually be unable to continue. We could just about get to a neutral harbour, if we were lucky."

The Captain turned towards his friend, a broad smile on his face.

"Well, Andras, you are now in charge. Sort it out."

"Thank you very much Sir," said Andras feelingly.

FOUR

The Captain rose with difficulty:

"I think I will have a rest and will leave you to it," he said, looking at the First Lieutenant. Clearly he did not want to embarrass his fellow officers while they decide what to do with him. They stood up and went together to the officers' mess.

All of the officers, with the exception of Mucha, who was Officer of the Watch on the bridge, sat down again. Lieutenant Mucha was still something of a stranger to them. When he came aboard the *'Eagle'* as the new gunnery officer, Dasay took one look at him and declared: "He looks like a bloody schoolteacher."

Round-shouldered, bookish with a scholarly attitude he certainly had the look of a schoolteacher about him, which was not surprising because, for the past eight years he had been one, at Sopot High School. A student of history and with a clear understanding of politics and the international situation, he was convinced that war with Germany was inevitable and that he would pre-empt the situation by joining the armed services. The Navy was his only choice as he had lived near the sea and ships all his life. As he knew nothing at all about guns and weapons, he thought it would be a good idea to learn a new skill, so volunteered for the gunnery training school. His ability to learn quickly enabled him to qualify rapidly, and his standing in the community persuaded the authorities to commission him. There was an urgent need for able officers.

"I've made up my mind what I think we should do," Andras declared, "but I would like to hear what you all have to say bearing in mind that we've got to get the Captain to a hospital as quickly as possible, so a small harbour on some isolated part of a coast is useless. And we've got to find somewhere where there is a naval harbour so we can get some quick repairs done. Piotr?" He looked to the senior lieutenant.

"Stockholm," came the quick reply, "sure to have a good hospital handy. And we believe the other damaged boats have gone to Sweden. We could avoid the possibility of internment by dropping him off the Swedish coast in a dinghy, or even ask the Swedes to come and pick him up. If we explained his state of health they would be sympathetic. After all, they are on our side. Aren't they?"

Tomasz's pale blue eyes which normally had a faraway look as if he was thinking about something else, looked disgusted.

"Have you given any thought how we would get him off the submarine into a dinghy or any other sort of boat for that matter? We also need a naval dockyard and I don't believe Stockholm has got one, it is a normal port, mainly for passenger ships."

"Riga is a possibility, but I don't know how helpful the Latvians would be," offered Andrzej. "They can be quite awkward. I'm not sure whether they have a naval dockyard with the right equipment. And I'm not sure how sympathetic they are to the Germans or how much they are under their control. All the possible places are between 300 and 400 kilometres away, say three to four days sailing at best, depending on the weather and what we might meet. We will have to stay submerged during the day and only go up in daylight if the weather is helpful, poor visibility etc."

The other officers gave Andrzej a quizzical look, wondering why he was so keen to state the obvious. He was the officer responsible for the smooth running of the submarine and, unknown to him, he was also the butt of much humour among the crew because of his habit of touching everything he passed in a proprietarily manner as he inspected the boat

"Nights are getting longer," Thomasz offered, helpfully.

"What's the weather forecast?" asked Thomasz.

Andrzej shrugged.

"No idea. As far as I know Slawomir hasn't picked up one for ages, seems they have something else on their minds," he said.

"Well, it's okay at the moment, cloudy and calm, but getting a bit cold," offered Tomasz as the last one to have been on the bridge. "Let's hope it stays that way."

"Tallinn," said Jersey suddenly and unexpectedly. "I've given it some thought and its the only possible choice. It is by far and away the best. It has a good harbour, a small naval dockyard as they have a good, but small fleet. I seem to remember that the Russians once had an agreement to use it as a naval base. There is bound to be a good hospital nearby and the Estonians are likely to be sympathetic to us, they don't like the Germans."

"Who does?" interposed Piotr, surprised by this sudden outburst from the usually quiet and normally reticent engineer. The other officers remained silent, considering what he had said.

"My thoughts entirely," said Andras, speaking for the first time since the discussion started. "It is not only ideal, but it is probably the only choice we have. We have to establish the criteria for seeking temporary asylum in a neutral port. Let's get Ryzard in, he will know the legal implications."

Ryzard, who seemed to have anticipated that he might be called upon, and had waited outside, quickly joined the discussion group. A long serving Chief Petty Officer he had a reputation throughout the boat as the 'man who knows everything' not in a boastful way, but as a matter of fact. He was self-educated and well-read and was knowledgeable about a number of subjects. He was also well known as a 'mess deck lawyer' in that he knew naval regulations inside out.

Ryzard was from Poznan and was always quick to start explaining that the city's origins went back to the beginning of the nation and it quickly became one of the two strongholds of the new Polish nation. While the other, Gniezno, weakened after a move south to Krakow, Poznan took on a status of its own and Ryzard always gave the impression that he had developed a status of his own.

Poznan suffered badly from the Swedish invasion in the mid-17th century, and then lost its Polish name completely when incorporated into Prussia and it became Posen although it still considered itself Polish. Ryzard was proud of the fact that in 1918 it threw out its German rulers and was reinstated as Poznan a Polish city. Ryzard knew the history of his city well and was more than prepared to bore anyone who would listen to the details.

He was also known by the crew as the 'professor'. He gained this reputation by accident while on the bridge one night with two lookouts and the Officer of the Watch. One of the lookouts had pointed out a very bright object in the sky exclaiming "look at that bright star".

"It's not a star," said Ryzard conversationally, "it's a planet, Venus, sometimes known wrongly as the evening star. It is one of the brightest objects in the sky, the second planet out from the Sun. You can tell it's a planet because it is not twinkling, the light is steady. Stars twinkle because they are such long distances away."

The lookout, Jake, looked at him with renewed respect.

"What are you, a bloody Professor?" he said, laughing.

"No I'm not, it's just something I know," said Ryzard. But the new nickname stuck Ryzard turned to Andras, glad once more of having the opportunity to use his knowledge.

"Under the Neutral Powers in the Naval War Agreement 1907, a belligerent warship can claim 24 hours asylum in a neutral port to carry out vital repairs to make it seaworthy, or land wounded or sick crew members. They can carry out only repairs that are absolutely necessary to make the ship seaworthy, but nothing which improves its fighting capability.

It is up to the neutral power to agree what repairs are necessary. A belligerent ship may not leave a neutral port until 24 hours after the departure of a merchant ship flying the flag of an adversary."

"Thank you," the First Lieutenant smiled, "I thought you'd have a rough idea."

"As far as I remember it," Ryzard continued, unabashed by the Captain's joke," under the Estonian Law of Neutrality, which they introduced last year, it is forbidden for armed submarines and warships of a warring power to enter Estonian territorial waters. But if submarines which, due to weather, or shipwreck or damage, are forced into forbidden territory they have to indicate their presence by international signals. They have to leave immediately their reason for their presence has been removed. I think that's right."

"You are a fountain of knowledge," said the Captain, putting his hand on Ryzard's shoulder, "very helpful."

"That's settled then, we'll make for Tallinn at best speed. What is it, Jersey?"

"Submerged five knots, I would suggest ten knots on the surface. I know we have to get there as soon as possible for the Captain's sake, but we have to look ahead and preserve fuel because we have no idea when we will be able to get any more," the engineer replied.

"Okay that sounds right, but keep me informed, especially

about fuel consumption, I will want continual reports and forecasts. When we get near Tallinn we will have to signal the authorities and explain our situation and hope they are sympathetic. You will now act as Second-in-Command. That's the only change I suggest." Piotr nodded in acceptance, it was an expected move.

Piotr, tall and slim with a thin face capped by a tight crown of fair hair, had the look of a superior *'Eagle'*. He did not stand and watch what was going on, he poised, his head still, but his eyes taking in everything that was going on. He said little and only spoke when he had something particular to say or contribute, and did not take part in the usual idle chatter in the mess or on deck. He was much respected by his fellow officers and the men and he, in turn, was devoted to both the Captain and Andras. The new acting Captain clapped his hands together: "Right, let's move. I will talk to the Captain and tell him our plans." He stood up, smiled at his colleagues and left.

Piotr, one of the most experienced officers on the submarine, decided to take up his new duties immediately and go the bridge to check with Mucha what was happening. He was extremely glad that, with extra responsibility, he could put his immediate past out of his mind.

A few days before *'Eagle'* sailed he had received a letter from his wife Marcia, who had gone to stay with her Mother on the ground that she was frightened by all the war talk. He could not remember when he had last received a letter. In fact, when he really thought about it, he remembered that he had never ever received a letter,. He could not think of anyone he knew who could write, or had anything important enough to write about.

It had never been an every day activity in his family. Come to think of it the question had never arisen. If you had something you wanted to say to someone, you said it when you next saw them, and that was more often than not later the same day.

It was in a rough looking envelope with his name on, and had obviously been pushed through the door, as the village in which he lived was so obscure that there was no local postal service. The writing was hurried, more a scribble. She was very sorry, really sorry, but she was sure he would understand. She had met someone else, no-one he knew. She had really fallen in love with him and love was something that just happened, you could not plan it. She wanted to marry him, but of course, that meant she needed a divorce. She supposed he would give her one. There was no point in being married if you did not love the other person. And he was away so much she was often very lonely.

His first reaction, after getting over the shock was "My God, I certainly will not. She's not going to have it that easy. I will fight her all the way." He had been thinking about it ever since, and had fluctuated between playing the hard 'over my dead body' man and a compassionate human being. He had not yet made a final decision.

His mind returned to the current situation. A man with strong views he often disagreed with Andras, but they always remained close friends. He was very pleased that Andras was now the acting Captain. The future was going to be very difficult, but he could not think of a better man to handle the difficulties.

* * *

Moving out of Gdansk Bay the *'Eagle'* headed north east. Meanwhile large numbers of German trawlers and patrol vessels were searching the water surface, and close formations of aircraft hovered above the sea. They forced the submarine to navigate in the deepest waters available. Very often the short hours in the middle of the night, spent on the surface charging batteries, were interrupted by the sudden appearance of German craft. It was a bright autumn moon which, although not yet half full, in a cloudless sky and with the sea as smooth as a mirror, gave plenty of illumination to help the enemy.

One night in the moon's rays the watch on the bridge of *Eagle* thought he saw, in the distance their sister ship *Vulture* - it could be the last sight they had of a Polish warship for a long time. Every man on the bridge turned his binoculars towards the black smudge, but it had disappeared before they could make any identification.

"What do you know about the Baltic?" Officer of the Watch Tomasz asked Jersey who was on the bridge trying to grab a breath of fresh air.

"I know that it is no place for a submarine to be with a war going on, the enemy on the south coast, nervous neutrals on the other sides and one of Poland's worst enemies at one end."

"Apart from that?" said Tomasz, smiling.

"It's got four large islands, but only Bornholm and Gotland will worry us. Average depth is around 30 to 60 metres, but it can be dodgy. The wind can get up without warning and cause trouble, particularly if it's from the East. It's got three large Gulfs, Finland, Bothnia and Riga, and it's Finland we are heading for. We'll pass two smaller islands to starboard, off the coast of Estonia," explained Jersey.

"That's all very comforting," Tomasz replied. "But after we have been to Tallinn. What then?"

"That's the problem. We can either wander around shooting at Germans until our weapons, fuel and food run out, or we can try and do the impossible and get out into the North Sea, between Denmark and Sweden, where the gap is about three miles wide and probably full of German warships."

"Let's not think about it," Tomasz declared.

* * *

Marcin came on to the bridge and approached Tomasz: "Shall I take over now?" he asked.

"I don't see why not," replied Tomasz sharply, "you've taken over everything else."

"I thought we were forgetting about that for the time being. We can sort it out when this is all over," Marcin said quietly.

"You may be able to forget it, but I can't," Tomasz snapped. "We're headed zero four five degrees, speed ten knots, Andras to be informed if anything is seen. There's nothing else you need know." Tomasz turned away, his handing over duties done.

Tadeus had been standing at the rear of the bridge getting a much needed breath of fresh air. He heard the exchange between the two men, and it took his mind back to a personal problem he had been trying, not to forget, but to subdue for as long as possible.

Some six months previously his father had died leaving his mother Irena, alone in her small house at Lipno some 25 kilometres from where he and his wife, Beata, lived at Torun. He called on his mother regularly, but when war became inevitable her solitude became a worry. He quietly devised a solution which he felt sure would solve the problem satisfactorily. His mother would come and live at his house, she and Beata would be company for each other, and he would not have to worry about them. It was an ideal plan, but like most logical solutions there were snags, some quickly seemed insurmountable.

At first it was the critical eye which Irena cast over Beata's domestic activities that caused the first trembles - "I would not clean it like that", "that's not the way I would do it", "he would not have to get his own drink if I was looking after him", were just a few of the unspoken thoughts that Tadeusz could read in his mother's eyes.

Then they became more vocal, followed by reciprocal

comment from Beata. Then Beata began to express her views, and arguments developed which became full scale rows. Sometimes when he visited them they were not speaking to each other, then they were living their separate lives and in separate rooms, then, remarkably and for no apparent reason, they were very close and ganged up against him when he put a foot wrong, then it was back on the roller coaster.

Now, thought Tadeusz, what would it be like at home. If they had lived through the German advance how would they live together? Knowing his wife and his mother and the contrariness of women, he was sure that they would be devotedly looking after each other with love and affection. He sighed heavily, he would never understand the workings of a woman's mind.

***

Suddenly the serenity of the evening, and the peace in Tadeusz's mind, was broken by the cry: "Aircraft approaching off the port bow."

"Dive, dive, dive!" shouted Marcin, urging the lookouts off the bridge and following Tadeusz, who was no more than an inch in front. The men tumbled down the ladder and slammed the hatch shut as the sea was fast approaching the rim of the bridge. The clatter of the crew racing to their posts gave the scene a look of panic, but in reality it was a well-rehearsed manoeuvre.

Within seconds there was complete silence in the submarine as the crew settled and it gradually sank into the calm waters below the surface. So far it had been a routine exercise, but suddenly, mental alarm bells rang, Something was seriously wrong. A dozen pair of eyes were recording the fact that the depth gauge instead of showing the submarine going deeper was indicating it was rising. It was being taken back to the surface where it would be clearly seem from the air.. The gentle pitching of the boat indicated it was nearing the surface, followed by a slight shudder as it broke through.

"Emergency crash dive," shouted Andras against the shrieking of the warning klaxon. Crew members, thrown about by the rapid changes in movement, struggled back to their posts, hot, bruised and baffled.

Switches were thrown, valves thrust open as nerves tightened. At first nothing happened, for what seemed an age, but in reality was only a matter of seconds. The submarine seemed to be remaining on the surface. But then with the crashing sound of water rushing into the ballast tanks as though a dam had burst, the depth gauge reacted like a thermometer thrown into a bowl of boiling water. It showed a frightening increase in the speed of the descent…10m… 20m… 30m… 40m… 60m and then, steady. An audible sigh of relief, as the crew exhaled their breath, which like the heavy rush of escaping air when an airtight door was opened, burst from 54 men.

"God knows what happened then," Andras announced to no-one in particular. "But she seems steady now. Bring her back up to 35 metres." In a more sedate manner the submarine began to rise as slowly the excitement settled down, and men shuffled in their positions to try and regain some comfort.

Andras calmly ordered half the crew to stand down, eat and rest; the other half stayed at their posts, but in greater control of both their duties and their emotions. His voice showed no sign of excitement or that anything untoward had happened.

* * *

Near the galley on the lower deck, which was comparatively quiet at this time, Kacek, sitting with his back to boxes of food, was approached by a very nervous looking Seaman Hreinski.

"Can I have a word with you?"

"Sure, what's it about?"
"It's a bit personal."
"So?"
"Could we go somewhere quiet?"
"What? Here?"
"There must be somewhere, over there, by the diesel compressor." They moved quietly to the equipment which, at that moment, was clear of other bodies.

"Well?" asked Kacek, "what's the problem?"
"I've got an itch, it's quite bad." came the reply from the worried seaman.
"An itch? Where?"
"Down below," Hreinski explained, mysteriously.
"Down below what?"
"It's on my old man.," said Hreinski with impatient embarrassment
"Your old man, do you mean your cock?"
"Yes."
"What sort of itch?"
"A bad one, it's there all the time, I can't stand it. It's all red. I think I have some sort of disease."

Knowing your record I'm not surprised," said Kacek.

Hreinski was well known for his sexual activities when on shore leave. He took great pleasure in boasting about it in great detail. His most famous story, told whenever the opportunity arose, was on returning to the ship with his face very badly scratched. No-one had asked him what had happened in case he told them. But he told them anyway. He insisted on relating how he had gone to bed with two women, made love to one of them, had a sleep and then made love to the other girl. The trouble was it was not the other girl, it was the same one again and the ignored female became a vixen, she was livid and attacked him with long finger nails.

"Let's have a look," said Kacek.

"Don't be bloody stupid you're not having a look it. It's private."

"Don't you be bloody stupid. How can I suggest what to do unless I've seen it. I know what they're like. I've got one too."

Reluctantly Hreinski turned his face towards the bulkhead and furtively removed it from his trousers.

"Christ", said Kacek after one quick look, "put it away quickly it will frighten the dolphins. That is bloody awful."

"What can I do?"

"I have no bloody idea. I would say the first thing to do is wash it, but we cannot spare the water. I would soak it in sea water if I were you, try and get a container full the next time some comes in. I'll give you some petroleum jelly to put on it and hope that will do the trick. But I'm not too confident. I'm not a bloody doctor," Kacek said crossly.

"But you're the medical orderly and you're supposed to look after us."

"I'm supposed to look after those who are genuinely ill. I don't look after people with broken weapons."

The two parted with an embarrassed Hreinski looking worried and miserable and Kacek looking mystified, but with a slight smile on his face. Everyone gets their comeuppance, he thought.

* * *

In the aft torpedo compartment where some 20 men were gathered awaiting events a voice exclaimed: "My bloody watch is broken. I can't wind it up."

"Worse things happen at sea," a comedian interjected.

"It's not a joke, I have to know the time, besides, it's a family heirloom." Seaman Grzegorz had ambitions to be a lawyer until events dictated otherwise. He was punctilious and slightly pompous like most of the profession.

"It doesn't matter a damn what time it is down here. We don't even know what day it is. What does it matter whether your bloody watch is broken, my bloody nerves are shattered, but I'm not shouting about it," declared Officer Cadet Eryk.

"Give it to Jan, he's a watchmaker in real life, ask him," came a more serious contribution.

Everyone looked at the telegraphist who was off duty. A 22-year-old full of energy with looks which were nothing special, but were not helped by a broken nose, which attempted to point in two directions at the same time, and failed in both. It had been won through a successful attempt to stop someone poaching one of his girlfriends. He had dark intelligent eyes which were constantly on the move taking everything in, missing nothing, and was rarely caught unawares."

It was true he came from a family of watchmakers. His father, his grandfather and his father before him and almost every other male member of the large family throughout history had been watchmakers. His joke, in fact his only joke, was that his family always had time on their hands.

Born in the small town of Szeczin in western Pomerania, he grew up in a rural community from which people rarely travelled. In fact, his mother and father had never even seen the sea even though it was less than 50 km away. This had not deterred him, when it seemed that conflict with Germany was not far away, to look towards the Navy as his contribution to defending his country and his family.

Whatever happened, he thought, the Navy would broaden his horizons. Of course, the family disapproved. What would happen to their watch making traditions, they asked, completely ignoring the fact that the war would probably end their traditional family life anyway.

But Jan did what he thought was the next best thing, and joined the Navy. He thought that watches and radios were in the same skill bracket, so he trained as a radio operator which would also give him some sort of authority.

"My family are the watchmakers, I'm not, I know very little about them. If you can't wind it up the spring has bust and there is nothing I can do about that."

"You might at least have a look at it and make sure it is the spring."

"Okay, pass it over."

He flicked open the back, tried the winder and looked up. "It is broken" he declared emphatically, "but there may be some hope. Without a magnifying glass I can't be sure, but it could be that the end of the spring has become detached. I could probably mend it if I had a hammer and chisel."

"A what!"

"Only joking. If I had a magnifying glass and a small pair of pliers I might be able to do something about it, but I would not think we had either of them on board."

"Why aren't you a watchmaker if it's a family business?" someone asked.

"Think about it. Everyone in the family, including the dog is into watchmaking. If my dog was lying at my feet now it would have sat up the minute you lot started talking about watches he'd scratch himself and start ticking. Nothing else matters. My mother and father are constantly talking about clocks and watches. They talk about them at every meal. If they are not talking about watches they are talking about people who are concerned with them. They probably timed themselves every time they had sex. They are both around 60 and they've never been to the sea even though they live within spitting distance. I heard a rumour that there was more to the world than Szeczin so when it looked certain that war was coming. I decided to volunteer for the Navy rather than wait to be conscripted into the Army. Then I trained as a telegraphist and volunteered for the submarine service in order to see the world, instead all I've seen is the sea, above and under it. I'm quite happy, but I do worry about my two younger brothers and what has happened to them," he added reflectively.

Silence fell as his audience also began to remember people they had to worry about too.

* * *

The next two days passed slowly with a constant watch either on the surface, or through the periscope, for any sign of an enemy ship, but the sea was empty. In and around the control room the torpedo officer, Tomasz, became more and more impatient that there was no work for his beloved torpedoes. He spent all his time walking round looking as if he wanted to find something to complain about.

It became a joke among the crew that he stroked them as if they were his children. Jake, ever the gambler, tried to persuade the men to bet on what Tomasz would touch first when he walked into the torpedo compartments. Few took him up. He was too lucky.

It was about 2100 hrs on a quiet and calm night in the eastern Baltic, a slight breeze rippled the surface as those on the submarine's deck had the rare pleasure of seeing the lights of civilisation flicker on the distant shore. It marked their arrival at the coast of Estonia. There was no noise of gunfire, no blistering explosions, no instant death. Those below were talking quietly, grabbing as much sleep as they could, or playing cards with gentle enthusiasm.

Tallinn, the capital of Estonia as well as its only major port, boasts a small, but important harbour. Established in the 12th century and claimed by both Denmark and Sweden in the past, it had been annexed by Russia in 1710 and for the next 100 years was the naval base of the Russian Baltic fleet. It knew about handling warships.

A small basin about a quarter of a mile square, it has two entrances both about 30 metres wide. Its major drawback is that in the middle of the harbour is shallow water covered by a small pile of rocks. Ships can only be tied up alongside the wharf. No vessel can anchor in the harbour itself.

It was time to signal the Estonian Government of their intentions.

"Would you give the Captain my compliments and ask him to come to the control room," Andras asked Marek who was acting as his messenger.

Looking slightly more relaxed and at ease the Captain walked in, greeting all those around him.

"We're off Tallinn, Sir. You wanted to know so we can send a signal and explain our presence."

"Good," the Captain replied, showing by his expression of relief that the end of his personal ordeal was almost over. "Send the following: *'This is the Polish submarine 'Eagle', Captain Henryk. We have a sick person on board who urgently needs hospital treatment and we have trouble with our engine. I request permission to enter port and seek 24hr asylum under the Geneva Convention.'*" Slawomir made a note and went off to carry out his orders.

Now it's a question of wait and see," said the Captain, looking at his First Lieutenant.

"I should not think we'll have a problem. They can hardly refuse a sick patient. The Estonians will be on our side, even if they can't say so in so many words," Andras replied.

Both men visualised the flurry of diplomatic activity there would now be in the Estonian corridors of power.

A comfortable calm fell over the submarine which had faced so many days of danger and fearful activity. It was half-an-hour before Jake, one of the lookouts, shouted: "Motor boat leaving the harbour. It has three men on board, two in uniform, one civilian."

"Call the Captain to the bridge," Piotr, Officer of the Watch ordered.

The Captain, trying to appear as normal as possible, clambered painfully up the ladder while all eyes were focussed on the small boat which bounced over the slightly choppy sea to the submarine.

It drew up alongside and one of the uniformed men threw a rope to a sailor on the deck of the submarine while another, obviously superior, judging by his gold braid and medals made as if to board.

"Wait," ordered the Captain. "You have not been given permission to come aboard. What do you want?"

"I have instructions to collect your request for asylum in writing. I have to have it in Polish and Russian," came the shouted reply. "Without it permission cannot be granted."

"Wait there. Why Russian?" The civilian shrugged.

The Captain, knowing the habits of the diplomatic corps, had already had the request prepared in Polish, German and Russian. Who knew who was really in control in Tallinn.

A small brown paper package was handed to the civilian and the motor boat turned and made its way slowly back towards the harbour. The waiting began again.

* * *

Andrzej, the senior lieutenant, a tall thin 32-year-old officer with several years of experience, took over as Officer of the Watch. His features were dominated by his narrow face and a thin, well designed, straight nose which pointed with great accuracy to a narrow pointed chin. His other main feature, was his known habit of examining every piece of equipment. Gambler Jake, would offer bets on which piece of equipment he would touch first when he entered a compartment. Although everyone knew that Jake never offered a bet unless he was sure of winning and would study his subject in great detail, his wager would often be taken up simply for the hell of it. Life was largely a boring routine with orders and instructions, so why not have a go now and then. After all, Jake could lose and the life would become even and more acceptable.

Andrzej checked the compass to ensure that the submarine was in its correct position, looked at the logbook to see if there was anything new he should know, relaxed, and turned to look across the water at the lights of Tallinn. It reminded him of civilisation and his home town of Slupske in Western Pomerania and this, in turn, reminded him of Mill Gate where he used to meet his wife when they were courting. The thought of his wife, brought back a feeling of guilt and memories of the unhappy weeks before the war when his wife left him. They had, after a discussion inspired by her, decided on a period of trial separation. As far as he knew no-one else was involved, certainly not on his side.

Life with him, she alleged, was boring and she wanted no more out of it. They had nothing of mutual interest any more. He had no time for her, all he thought about was his blasted Navy. She had her own interests, her school teaching and relevant activities from which she got more satisfaction. He had suggested that maybe the possibility of war made his interest in the Navy forgivable, but clearly, it was not. He had not really thought much about her afterwards. Talk of war and preparation, or the lack of, it dominated discussions. Had she decided to leave him to teach him a lesson?

Was it her way of getting her own back on him? He knew in his heart that he had not given her the love and attention she deserved as a wife. He did not think she had found someone else. His single-mindedness and his devotion to the Navy was probably the real reason that the marriage had fallen apart. He sighed deeply, wondering what was happening to her now. Slupske was a small town with little of strategic value in or around it, so probably the Germans had ignored it. He knew he was kidding himself. It did not matter what Slupske was like or whether it had any strategic value. One thing over-rode all that, for his wife, Marcia, came from a Jewish family and Germany's attitude to the Jewish race was well understood.

He shook himself. It was not something to dwell on at this moment. The *'Eagle'* was in trouble and much would depend upon him.

* * *

It was 0130 hrs when another call from a lookout announced that the motor boat was on its way back. Again it had two uniformed men and a civilian on board. On arrival the civilian passed a document to a submarine deckhand who passed it up to the Captain on the bridge. He looked quizzically at Andras before he opened it and read it.

"We have permission from the Estonian authorities to enter port," he announced with a look of relief. He thanked the civilian messenger who showed no reaction or interest and the motor boat turned and went back to Tallinn.

"Well, I suppose the next thing is to go into Tallinn and make the arrangements to enter. Andras, you come with me. Piotr, take control and let no-one on board," the Captain instructed. The two men, accompanied by Warrant Officer Kazik, boarded the submarine's motor boat and headed for the Estonian port in silence, the Captain relieved that his physical ordeal was nearly at an end; Andras considering the trials and tribulations that were facing him.

The Commander-in-Chief of the Estonian Navy and the Polish Military Attaché were in the latter's office waiting together with a bevy of blank, expressionless faces of inferior rank.

"I can confirm that you have permission to enter port and leave after your compressor has been repaired," said the

Estonian officer. "But there is one small problem. We have a German freighter in port at the moment. She is due to leave tomorrow morning. Under the Convention on the Rights and Duties of Neutral Power in Naval War a vessel of one belligerent power cannot leave port until 24 hours after a vessel of the other belligerent power. I'm sorry. I hope you understand."

"If that is the law that is how it will be," said the 'Eagle's Captain.

"Now," said the Estonian in a matter-of-fact manner, "we must get you to hospital, you look extremely ill and I am sorry there has been a necessary delay. And we must arrange the repair of your compressor," he added with a friendly smile.

The Captain, the relief that his physical ordeal was nearing its end clashing with the heart break of having to abandon his ship in its time of need, turned to his First Lieutenant. "Well, Andras, that's it then. You are now officially the Captain of the *'Eagle'*. " I wish you the very best of luck and success in the future."

Andras took his friend's hand with both of his and looked into his eyes. "I sincerely hope that they look after you properly in hospital and you make a full return to good health. I am sure they will," he said, fighting his own emotions. "It has been a very enjoyable experience working with you. You have taught me a lot. I hope we meet again when this terrible business is over."

He stepped back and saluted his Captain, who returned the salute. They both found it difficult to say more.

At that moment the Estonian doctor took his arm gently. "Let's get you where we can start looking after you; you've had a rough time." He turned to Andras: "Don't worry we will look after him.

The two Polish officers shook hands again and the Captain left the room.

Andras turned to the Polish military attaché. "I must get back to the *'Eagle'* and bring her in.

With an Estonian pilot Andras and Kazik returned to the

submarine. The pilot then took charge of bringing the *'Eagle'* into port, giving instructions to the helmsman Cazegorz. Andras moved close to him, and in a low voice muttered. "Make a good note of the way in, it may be useful on the way out."

Once in the harbour the *'Eagle'* was greeted by a tug which took it in tow. The crew were mortified to see the jagged rocks in the centre of the harbour and the fact that it was impossible to anchor away from the jetty.

Piotr, now the First Lieutenant, was on the bridge with Andrzej, he turned and pointed out: "Have you noticed that we are being towed to a space in the furthest, most obscure, corner. We are not being taken to an open jetty space."

"Yes," replied Andrzej," and have you also noticed that there is a gunboat over there and five destroyers and two submarines alongside three sides of the basin?"

Ryzard, who was also on the bridge taking their situation in, pointed to the berth they were about to pass: "That's an interesting sight." he said, pointing to what was obviously the German freighter that was supposed to be leaving the next day.

"Can you see they have painted the smoke stack and blocked out the name of the shipping company. The word 'Hamburg' has also been painted over, but is still visible.

The Nazi flag has obviously been removed, because it does not have a national flag of any sort. And, incidentally, I can't see any preparations being made to sail." The three men looked at the enemy ship, each wondering about what it could mean.

The *'Eagle'* as they had deduced, was towed to the berth furthest away from the entrance. It was secured by four thick wire hawsers to the jetty, by another to a destroyer and a sixth held the bow to an anchor in the harbour.

"They want to make absolutely certain that we cannot accidentally break away," said Piotr, laughing.

***

FIVE

The mood within the submarine improved dramatically. The Captain was now in good hands with, they had said, an excellent chance of a full recovery; the compressor was being repaired, the evaporator replaced and a return to the Baltic to continue the fight against the enemy would soon be resumed. Although the Captain had played his role to the full despite his illness, he had been a weak link, always in everyone's thoughts when they should have been concentrating on the war. Now, they felt, the '*Eagle*' was once again a complete fighting unit. It was ready for battle without distraction.

Even Slawomir was seen to smile, although no-one could figure out the reason. Maybe it was because good Estonian food was being brought on board and he might be able to put on some weight. In fact he was, as usual, thinking about food and the old women at home who brought the food to the table. There was usually a meat paste made of corn, flour and water, and a piece of thick pork sausage encased in the entrails of a pig, and a pitcher of sour milk and thick black bread and cheese and radishes. Then there would be sunflower seeds in honey, and hard wheat cakes, and apples, and pierogi, boiled dumplings of unleavened dough, stuffed with varying ingredients. Other food, such as sweet potato, or cheese, together with vegetables, sauerkraut, mushrooms, spinach and blueberries, would all be piled on the same plate. He sighed with happiness at the thought of such a feast. One could dream.

For the first time for several days the atmosphere in the submarine was comparatively pleasant, the smell of ageing vegetables, diesel fumes and body odours was now diluted by an infiltration of fresh air percolating through the hatch. For the men, after hours spent confined in sultry heat, it could almost be described as luxurious,

The fact that leaving Tallinn was now on the cards had the usual effect on Jake who was always quick to seize an opportunity.

"I'm going to run a book on what time we leave Tallinn," he declared. All those within hearing distance groaned. "Everyone puts a day's pay on the time they think we will pass through the entrance on our way out. Who is nearest gets the prize."

"What's the prize" asked a sceptical Dasay.

"Ninety-five percent of the money bet."

"What happens to the other five-percent?" Dasay queried with a suspicious look.

"I keep that for running costs and organising it."

"What bloody running costs? Are you renting the submarine as your headquarters?" Yarwin suggested.

"Don't be damn silly. I'll have to keep records and organise the pay out. The organiser always gets a commission," Jake explained seriously.

"What happens if no-one guesses right?" Yarwin persisted.

"I keep the records and the money goes on the next bet." Jake responded reasonably.

"For Christ's sake Jake, stop taking us for a crowd of bloody idiots," Dasay snapped angrily. "We need a bit of fun" he said, turning to the others. "But I reckon Grzegorsz should organise it, he wants to be a lawyer so he can work out the rules. It will be good practice. If no-one gets it right all bets are off." It was a surprise to hear Dasay agreeing to anything, so the others nodded their assent.

"Like hell," Gregorsz said with emphasis. "I'm not an accountant."

"No, we trust you," Waldemar told him with a friendly smile. "and Jake's a born crook. All you have to do is keep a record of who gives you a time. You will decide with the Officer of the Watch's help what time we actually go through and who wins."

Gregorsz gave Waldemar a pleading look, but he agreed, against his better judgement. "Okay," said Jake cheerfully as if no-one had disagreed with him and ignoring the insult.

"Let's go ahead. We came in early on Saturday, they said we could stay 24 hours, that takes us to Sunday, and then they said we must wait until after the German ship had gone, Assuming it goes today, that takes us to Monday so I reckon around noon Monday. I'll say, definitely, 1200 noon Monday."

"Won't be that quick," suggested Yarwin, "they're bound to bugger about, they always do. I'll say 1700hrs Monday afternoon."

"I've no bloody idea," declared Waldemar, "and I think you are all mad anyway, but I'll go halfway between you two and say 1430."

"We can't let a potential officer win this," said Dasay with insincere humour against Yarwin. "I don't have any faith that it will go without a major hitch, they are all so bloody incompetent. Waldemar is right, they'll cock it up, but properly, so I'll say 2100 hrs.

"The others began to join in quickly with various times between 1100hrs and 2200hrs. All were quite definite in their selections and Gregorsz wrote down the times carefully, repeating the time suggested to everyone so there would be no doubt. He then had second thoughts, knowing his shipmates, and made them all put their signature next to the time they suggested.

The discussion broke up in a series of individual debates

over the times picked or what minor delay could throw out their calculations. They had not enjoyed themselves so much for weeks.

*　*　*

The high spirits were soon dampened.

Piotr, the duty Officer of the Watch gave the alarm. He saw a small group of military men marching purposefully down the jetty towards the submarine.

"Officer and armed men approaching," he shouted," get the Captain to the bridge."

Andras, in his new role, came onto the bridge pulling on his jacket. The squad came to a halt by the gangway.

"I have an urgent message for you," said the Estonian who, judging by his gold braid and medals, was quite important, but he wasn't the man they had dealt with earlier.

He walked up the gangway and demanded: "Are you the Captain?" Andras nodded and took the document.

"I am instructed to tell you that your submarine is to be interned," said the Estonian using an unnatural official voice, as if announcing the death of some notable personality. "It will be disarmed immediately. The officers will be escorted to the barracks and the crew will be put in confinement. No argument is possible."

Andras looked at the document in shocked disbelief.

"Argument is very possible," he snapped. "We have your written agreement that we can stay 24 hours when our repairs are complete and then, if the German ship leaves, another 24 hours after that. You cannot go back on that decision which was agreed by your Commander-in-Chief and witnessed by the Polish Military Attaché."

"Circumstances change, as you will see," replied the Estonian smugly, looking over Andras's shoulder.

Andras and his officers who had gathered around him in a gesture of support, turned to see where he was looking. Two Estonian destroyers and several gunboats had turned their guns, manned and aimed at the *'Eagle'*.

"This is bloody disgraceful," snapped Andras, "I thought the Estonians were our friends. Fine bloody friends." The threat from the Estonians was clear, if unspoken.

"There is nothing you can do," the Estonian said with a false smile of sympathy. "The decision has been made. You are to be disarmed. We will start removing your torpedoes immediately. I am ordered to take the ship's papers and instruments with me when I leave."

"And if we don't comply you will blow us out of the water, killing most of us. I cannot believe this is an Estonian decision," snapped Andras looking directly at the officer who was now looking at the ground with embarrassment.

Andras gave Piotr a knowing look. "Piotr, please take our visitor and his companions to the control room while I get what he wants." The party went below while Andras moved swiftly to his cabin, gathered the confidential papers, tore them up into small pieces and stuffed them into a large envelope. He turned to Eryk who had come up behind him in case he was needed.

"Go up to the stern hatch as quickly as you can and thrown these in the harbour on the starboard side so no-one sees you." Eryk moved quickly and quietly away.

Andras gathered up other papers of no importance, put them in an official envelope and took them to the control room. The Estonian had already gathered up the charts, the sextant and other instruments and handed them to the armed guard with the envelope.

"Take these to headquarters," he ordered them.

On the jetty heavy vehicles with lifting gear had already been drawn up alongside the submarine, loading hatches had been opened, and a working party moved into position. Armed guards had been posted by the gangways, fore and aft.

* * *

It was a very depressed group of officers who gathered in the control room when the Estonians had withdrawn.

"What's their excuse?" Andras asked Jersey. "If they have one."

"Oh! Yes, they've got one. In fact they've probably got two. The first one is based on the pompous sounding Protocol of Neutrality allegedly signed by the Baltic States in 1938, although I've never heard of it; and Article 16 of the 11th Convention on the Rights and Duties of Neutral Powers in Naval War 1907. Briefly they say that we can stay for 24 hours only for repairs to be carried out. But they also say that there has to be a 24 hour gap between the departure of ships of conflicting powers. That means that we have to give the German freighter *'Thalatta'* a 24 hour start when it sails. That, in turn, means that if the German ship leaves tomorrow, when we are due to go, we have to wait another 24 hours and that means we will be here for 48 hours and that breaks the original 24 agreement for us."

"We know all that," Andras interrupted impatiently.

"But that's not all," Jersey continued unperturbed, "The Protocol states that no submarine can enter a neutral port unless the weather is so bad it cannot sail, or the technical repairs for which it seeks asylum make navigation impossible. Our cracked compressor and broken evaporator do not affect our navigational capabilities so we should not have been allowed it in the first place."

"It's diplomatic gobble-de-gook," snapped Piotr. "They shouldn't be allowed to get away with it. The C-in-C knew what was wrong when he let us in."

"I don't think it has anything to do with the Estonians," declared Ryzard who had been invited to join the discussion. "You've got to remember that Estonia is a small independent country sandwiched between two great powers, Germany and Russia. Estonia has a common border with Russia and to all intents and purposes Poland has already been defeated, unless there's a bloody miracle. As far as the Estonians are concerned Russia is a greater danger to them, therefore they do not wish to upset the Germans who may be persuaded to protect them if necessary. Most Estonians are known to be pro-Polish and they obviously are, for when we entered harbour they should have put all our officers in a shore base immediately, that's standard practice."

"So you're saying the Estonians have been forced to change their minds about us to get German support?" asked Piotr.

"Absolutely. Slawomir tells me that there has been a radio report that the Russians have already alleged we've sunk a Russian ship in the Gulf of Finland. This is a pretext to enable them to demand that Estonia lets the Russian fleet use their naval bases."

"I do not know whether anyone noticed," Tomasz pointed out," that when the Estonians left they removed the Polish flag from our bow pole. Almost immediately the *'Thalatta'* hoisted the Nazi flag,

"Well, all that is very interesting, "Andras interrupted, "the main question is, what do you suggest we do now?"

"Escape," said Piotr emphatically.

"Easier said than done," said Tomasz, "it looks impossible."

"Don't forget we do the impossible," Jersey replied. Each one of them mentally looked back at what they had done so far. It gave them confidence.

Andras looked at his officers with a feeling of pride. With this lot we might do it, he thought.

"The first thing we must do is to try and keep as much

equipment and as many weapons as we can. Piotr and I, with Andrzej, will work out an escape plan. We'll meet later to check what we still have on board and how to get out. Off you go," he added, looking at Tomasz, Jersey and Mucha, "and save what you can."

* * *

A naval officer arrived with two men to oversee the unloading some of the submarine's torpedoes.

They moved with confidence and surety towards one of the torpedoes on the standby racks.

"What the hell are you doing," the Tomasz shouted angrily, stamping towards them. "We are taking out these torpedoes," said the Estonian "We have already moved some of the others."

"For Christ's sake you can't touch those. They haven't been defused."

"We took the others," the Estonian said, motioning to his men to start work.

"They had been defused. I haven't had time to do these."

"What difference does it make?"

"Let me tell you what bloody difference it makes," said Tomasz, his anger rising, "if you bang or drop one of these, without them being defused, they will blow and if one goes the vibration will set off the others. You, me and everyone else will be spread across Tallinn like a pudding hit by a sledgehammer in a matter of seconds."

The Estonian backed away nervously, alarmed by Tomasz's warning

"How long will it take to defuse them?" the officer asked impatiently, seemingly unconcerned about his men's safety.

"An hour or so and I'm not doing it now, I am too tired and I need to have a very steady hand. I will do it early on Monday." said Tomasz as firmly as he could.

"You could do it tomorrow."

"Tomorrow is Sunday. I do not know about you, but I am a good Catholic and I do not work on Sunday. We have a church service in the morning under Polish Navy Standing Orders, and we dare not ignore those, and we have to relax the rest of the day," replied Tomasz, looking straight into the eyes of his adversary.

"You are not under Polish Standing Orders now, you are our prisoners, you do what we say," came the authoritative response. "I am under instructions to remove these torpedoes today and I have to obey my orders and so do you."

"Do I have to talk to your Admiral and explain how unreasonable you are being? We are supposed to be under your protection seeking asylum. This is not a very good way to show friendship. You don't have to worry, I swear to God, and I am very religious, that the torpedoes will still be where they are now on Monday morning. I will do everything that has to be done at that time."

The Estonian seemed doubtful, he was not used to his sort of job. He shrugged and ordered his men ashore.

Tomasz followed them to the gangway, his heart still pumping rapidly. I wonder where they would put a fuse on a torpedo he asked himself.

* * *

Food and his continual inability to put on weight was the last thing on Slawomir's mind. He was peering at the radio equipment, closely watched by his Estonian guard. He poked his screw driver around, tested wires, checked joints and plugs and stood back sighing. He looked at the guard with a look of mock despair. The guard looked back sympathetically, although he seemed to be not sure what he was being sympathetic about.

"This is not easy," Slawomir explained chattily. "A radio is a very complicated piece of equipment. Do you know anything about radios and electricity?" The guard shook his head.

Slawomir began to work slowly, removing the cover and sorting out his instruments. He stepped forward and carefully detached two wires and studied them closely, following them with his fingers back to their source at the base of the radio.

"Hold these," he ordered, pushing the wires into the Estonian's hand. The Estonian took them and peered at them with interest. Slawomir studied the radio equipment again. With his right hand he placed his screw driver on a small screw at the base of the equipment. With his left hand, out of the Estonian's sight, he flicked a switch.

There was a sharp crack, a burst of blue smoke and a yell of pain from the Estonian who had been electrocuted. He stepped back holding his injured hand a look of baffled astonishment on his face.

Slawomir looked at him in horror.

"You have broken the bloody thing," he shouted angrily.

The Estonian looked at his throbbing and smoke blackened hand. He was expecting sympathy, but what he got was intense anger.

"Me?"

"Yes, by holding those two wires you fool," said Salwomir with a face full of outrage.

"But you told me to," came the shocked reply.

"I did not mean hold them both in one hand you idiot. Do you not know anything about electricity? I meant hold them like this," Slawomir demonstrated by holding them carefully in each hand.

The Estonian, still gripping his injured hand like a man greeting himself warmly, looked totally mystified.

"This is very serious," said Slawomir with gravity. "I will have to speak to your superior officer."

The Estonian looked crestfallen. His world was falling apart. He could see trouble coming and his superior was not a very understanding man. He would enjoy making his life a misery.

Slawomir, seeing the Estonian's dilemma suddenly became sympathetic.

"It cannot be helped, it's too late now. I do not want you to get into trouble," he said kindly. "I will not report you, but I will have to check the radio and repair the damage so that I can dismantle it professionally. It would be best if you go and have medical attention. An electric shock can cause a number of problems, especially to the heart. Go and make sure you are all right. Explain at the hospital that you have had an accident. I will continue while you are away."

The Estonian, relieved that there was unlikely to be any disciplinary action, hurried off to seek attention. Slawomir heaved his own sigh of relief. At least he had saved the radio. He would now have to repair the wires on the air conditioning unit.

* * *

Anyone seeking the romance of the sea would not even consider looking in a ship's engine room, particularly that of a submarine. Even a machinery loving engineer who sees beauty where any sensible person sees only a mass of pistons, valves, and dials in an overpowering diesel oil dominated atmosphere, would find it difficult.

It is impossible to stand back and admire the scene because the observer becomes part of it when they enter the engine compartment. A diesel engine stands on either side of the central gangway, no more than two metres apart, grease and oil glistening off every part seemingly indicating its smooth running ability. It is a blessing for the stokers who work there that the engines cannot be used when the submarine is submerged, electric motors take over, because the noise of the pistons making several hundred revolutions a minute, is overpowering.

This was the scene where the third act of the retention drama was enacted.

"You are not working on the engine," the Estonian officer overseeing the operation pointed out to Jersey.

"No."

"Why not?"

"Why?"

"You are supposed to be disabling it."

"Why?"

"You are being disarmed and interned. It is part of the Order."

"The engine is not an armament. It is not included in the Order."

"It is," replied the Estonian with some emphasis, thrusting a document towards Jersey.

"Where does it say the engine has to be disabled?" Jersey asked handing the document back.

The Estonian's language ability was enough to enable him to understand what was being said, and to make himself understood, but his ability to read Polish or English was non-existent. He studied the paper knowledgeably.

"It says here, disabled," he pointed triumphantly at the word in one of the paragraphs.

"Disabled is not the same as dismantled," Jersey informed him. "The submarine is already disabled now because it is tied up in your harbour and you have taken all our instruments."

The engineer heaved a sigh of exaggerated frustration. "There's no point, we can't go anywhere, our ship is tied up to one of your warships. Besides, it's going to be here for ages and you might have to move it to another berth." He wiped his hands on a greasy cloth to show that that was the end of it.

"If we want to move it we will tow it," the Estonian replied with emphasis.

"Anyway," the engineer told him. "I don't agree that it has to be disabled and apart from that I cannot do it without the manual." replied the engineer.

"What manual."

"Another sigh. *'The Engineer's Manual of the Sulzer 6QD42 diesel engine'*, "he said in capitals. "I cannot work without it."

"Get it," the Estonian snapped irritably.

"I cannot."

"Why not?"

"Because it was taken away with all the documents yesterday," the engineer said with some satisfaction.

"Why do you need it, you should know all about your engines by now. You don't have to have instructions to take something apart you just do it."

"It's not that easy," Jersey laughed, "it's a question of the way you disable it. You have to remove certain parts in a special order. It has to be done in sequence otherwise you can't do it. If you move the wrong one out of sequence it stops you removing those around it because the toggle switches become entangled, and it is one hell of a job to disentangle them. I've known it take several hours and you have to put everything back before you take it apart. Damned annoying."

The Estonian looked mystified, he had no idea what Jersey was talking about.

The Engineer looked at him with a degree of pity in his eyes. "Look," he said patiently, "the parts have to be moved in order because they are assembled sequentially. It really is very complicated. If you bring the manual back I will show you and do it on Monday."

"You have been an engineer long enough, you should know the order in which they should be removed."

"I don't. I don't dismantle the engine as a matter of habit. In fact, I have never done it. It is always done in harbour by fully qualified dismantlers who have the right equipment. But if you get me the manual I will try and do it with the equipment I have."

"I will get the manual now and you can do it tomorrow," said the Estonian, starting to walk away.

"No, I won't. I am a devout Catholic and I do not work on Sunday."

"Catholics in Estonia work on Sunday."

"Polish Catholics don't." Jersey retorted, privately asking the Almighty for forgiveness.

"But you work on the engines on Sunday when you are at sea."

"That's maintenance, not proper work. Sorry."

The Estonian was lost for words. There was no way of making the engineer do what he was told, except the threat of violence which would not work

"Look, I know it is bad for you," said Jersey, trying to be conciliatory. "But it doesn't matter whether the engine is dismantled today, on Sunday or on Monday. We are now tied up to your warships, fore and aft so we can't go anywhere."

The despondent Estonian shrugged his shoulders and walked away in exhausted despair.

* * *

The emotional switchback, which had thrown the crew in every direction since the *'Eagle'* left its base at Gdynia, from anger at the German invasion, determination as they realised what lay ahead, fear as they gently slid their way through two minefields, deep concern as the Captain's health declined, hope as they finally reached Tallinn, euphoria as they were given permission to enter harbour, and relief when a period of asylum was granted, now turned again to anger at the duplicity of the Estonians.

Their anger was mingled with the sadness of what this could mean to them and their families. As long as they were at sea, still at war, there was hope, however ill-founded, that everything might turn out all right in the end. But if they were interned that was the end of the war for them, probably the end of their freedom forever if the Russians took over Estonia as seemed likely.

When the crew, faced with possible internment, wanted to take strong action, Warrant Officer Kazik was quickly on the scene to calm them down. He emphasised their perilous position, but pointed out that the officers were already taking a positive attitude to future action and would need the full support and trust of the crew.

A professional sailor who did everything by the book, Kazik would have been happier serving on a surface ship such as a destroyer where routine and discipline were the way of life. But he had volunteered for the submarine service because he had worked out that if war came the Polish Navy would not last long against the might of the German fleet, while submarines would at least have a chance of fighting back.

He found it difficult to get used to the relaxed atmosphere of the *'Eagle'* where the crew were a closely knit team with rank only marginally important and relations between officers and men more relaxed and informal. Born in Lodz, once the centre of the Polish textile industry, which had a bad reputation of strikes and demonstrations, he was not afraid to say what he thought, and tried to come down hard on any example of indiscipline. Gradually, however, the enthusiasm of the crew, who recognised what was right and what was wrong and what well worked together, began to soften him. The moment of being sorry for themselves, angry and anxious to take action lasted only minutes after Kazik had spoken.

Andras, closely watched by the Estonian guards, spoke to the crew in small groups so they would not be overheard. He realised that most of the guards could not understand Polish or English, but he did not want to take the chance. He quickly found out that the idea of escape received overwhelming support.

"The first task, of course, is to work out how this could be achieved, what is needed to be done and how to do it." Andras explained to the leaders of each group.

"Piotr, Chief Petty Officer Ryzard, and Mucha have been given the task of sorting out the details, Piotr as First Lieutenant, Ryzard because of his technical knowledge," he explained.

"Mucha is included in the group because he is popular with the men and will have little to do as Gunnery Officer because with the Estonians removing the breech from gun, it is useless. The gunnery team of Tabbert, Tadeusz and Grzegorz will be responsible for silencing the Estonian guards when the time comes. I've included Grzegorz because I'm told he has a very effective right fist. The guards should either be knocked out or tied up, no way should they be killed," Andras continued.

Tabbert was delighted to be given the chance to literally strike a blow for the *'Eagle'* and put one of the guards out of action. Like Kazik, a professional sailor all his working life, he was wedded to the Navy. He had served on gun-boats and destroyers and had volunteered for the submarine service because he wanted to be an important part of a small team rather than a cog in a bigger piece of machinery.

An even tempered man he had never been known to lose his temper and rarely get angry. He had a wiry frame, a pale face with sunken cheeks and close cropped hair which made him look unhealthy, but in reality he was fit and full of energy. But he had a warm, nature and was well liked by the crew. His major idiosyncrasy was that he was rarely seen without a pipe sticking out of his mouth. No-one objected, even in the close confines of the submarine, because the redeeming feature was that it was never alight. He found comfort in simply sucking it all day. Only on rare visits on deck would he actually put precious tobacco in it and produce smoke.

He was extremely proud of the *'Eagle's'* gun team, as well-trained professionals even though it had never been in action. He was quite sure that. with Tadeus and Marcin, there would be no chance of the Estonian guards giving the alarm.

Mucha's first surprise on joining the submarine had been to see a face he vaguely recognised. It turned out to be Officer Cadet Yarwin who had been a pupil at his school. He seemed to remember there was a problem, but could not immediately recall what it was.

"This is a surprise. I certainly did not expect to find you on a submarine," Mucha told him. "I'm glad to see you."

"Thank you Sir. It certainly was not my aim after leaving school, but events left little choice. I'm very happy to see you." His warm welcome hid mixed feelings. In one way he felt that seeing his old school teacher back in his life restored some reality to it. On the other hand his last experience with Mucha had not been a happy one. It was when he was thrown out of the school for cheating in the exams and Mucha, the senior teacher, had performed the coup-de-grace and sent him packing.

"I really am pleased to see you," repeated Mucha, confirming his first greeting because he had recalled the events. "I thought you were pretty useless at school and would come to no good. But I find you fighting for your country and working hard to get a commission. You have certainly learned your lesson. Well done!" Yarwin smiled and walked away sighing with relief and feeling an inch or two taller.

The planning group stood silently as each member tried to work out what needed to be done, and who should carry out the tasks. Suddenly Ryzard looked up: "I've just thought of something which will make life much easier," he said in a triumphant voice.

The others looked at him in anticipation.

"I've had something at the back of my mind for some time, but I could not pin it down," Ryzard said excitedly. "I knew there was something I had missed and could not recall it. It's been worrying me for some time. Now I know. That equipment at the end of the jetty, about 60 metres away, is clearly an electrical generator. It's the sub-station that provides all the electricity for the dockyard. Put that out of action and you plunge the whole place into darkness and cause chaos and panic."

His colleagues looked at him in amazement. Piotr looked at him steadily, the implications being dissected in his mind, Mucha sucked on his pipe reflectively, as usual, looking for snags.

"But how do we cut it," asked Piotr.

"Easy, one bloody good blow with an axe."

"But that will electrocute whoever cuts it?" asked Mucha logically.

"Not as long as the axe has a wooden handle," Ryzard explained. He had expected unquestioning enthusiasm and was disappointed by the calm reaction. He knew, however, that his colleagues were only trying to ensure that nothing could go wrong.

"Who would we use?" Piotr asked.

"Obviously, Marcin, he's got the strength to make sure one blow would do it."

"When would we do it?" Mucha persisted.

"About five minutes before we start to leave," Ryzard explained. "It would only take him around fifteen seconds to run back. The dockyard will be quiet at that time of night. It should not be too difficult for him to get there unseen and, once he's done it, they'll have a lot to think about."

"What about the sentry?"

"He would have been relieved of his duties," Piotr replied mysteriously. After thinking about it Ryzard decided not to ask.

Giving Janwyn the task of pretending to fish so that the depth of water beneath the submarine could be determined was, his colleagues saw, a clever character casting. A pleasant and quiet man he fitted exactly into the scene. When all was peaceful below he would present a hunched figure pouring over a book. His dark hair was tousled which, on a warship with proper discipline, would have been deemed too long. His blue chin gave the appearance that he was always in need of a shave and added to his dishevelled appearance.

He was a great reader and studied a number of subjects, but he was also a good example of the saying 'a little knowledge is a dangerous thing' for he would expound at length and in great detail on subjects about which he had only sketchy basic knowledge. As a result of this he was in constant argument with Robert and Ryzard, who – according to him - did know what they were talking about.

"I seem to remember," he announced seriously, after being told what his task was, "that there are about 20 species of fish in this part of the Baltic, but I think I will bait the line to catch cod and herring in this case."

"What the hell are you talking about," snapped Dasay. "You are only pretending to catch fish, you're supposed to be checking the depth of the bloody water."

"Yes, but you have got to look as though you know what you are doing otherwise you might give the game away."

"You clod. What do you think, that a sentry is going to watch you and then raise the alarm because you're using bait to catch a bloody whale, when you should be fishing for sprats?"

"Now you are being stupid," said Janwyn.

"Me being stupid? All you have got to do is drop a weighted line in and check the depth. Even a moron like you should be able to do that." Dasay replied impatiently. Janwyn felt that further argument was beneath him.

Leading Seamen Dasay and Lukasz and Officer Cadets Eryk and Maryk were given the job of cutting the mooring lines at a given time. It immediately became a competitive matter. The two lower ranks determined to cut their ropes more quickly and efficiently than the two prospective officers.

Artor's job was to incapacitate the crane used to off-load torpedoes. Chief Petty Officer Artor was an angry man. But it was anger which he kept from the crew, both the officers and the men. He was angry because he was still a non-commissioned Chief Petty Officer, even though he had been in the Navy for 12 years. He was convinced he should have been promoted and given a commission before now. His anger was exacerbated by the fact that his posting to the *'Eagle'* was at the same rank. It was not the first time he had not got what he considered to be his just desserts.

At school he was never given the approbation he believed he had earned. When one of the school's most popular boys was generously congratulated for earning 95 percent in a maths exam, but no mention was made of the fact that Artor had also got 95 percent.

When he was helmsman on a destroyer in the midst of one of the worst Baltic storms for years, he was awarded a quiet 'well done' from the Captain, but when he went below into his mess someone remarked 'so-and-so' did bloody well on the wheel. When Artor pointed out that he was him on the wheel at the time and not 'so-and-so' the conversation ended.

His only consolation now was that with a war on, and casualties high, the chances of promotion were much improved. But here he was, stuck on an isolated submarine in the middle of the Baltic Sea with not much to look forward to. And those who should be the ones to promote him were back at base, and probably dead. He was determined that if anyone carried out his task well, it would be Chief Petty Officer Artor.

He was, in fact, a popular member of the crew. Most of

those who met him for the first time described him as a typical sailor, relaxed and easy going, he walked with a typical sailor's roll. Of medium height and with an open, pleasant face, he was rarely flustered, whatever the crisis. He got some satisfaction from the fact that he had been given the hardest job of all, because it was agreed that the crane had to be put out of action as soon as possible, in broad daylight, to stop the Estonians unloading any more torpedoes.

"It's not going to be easy," Andras declared when he met Piotr and Artor.

"It is not going to be easy, it is not going to be impossible either," Piotr added optimistically.

"Well it can't be impossible because it has got to be done. We need a way of getting Artor onto the jetty and into the crane vehicle without the driver seeing him," Andras mused.

"If I may say so, Sir," Artor interrupted. "I think I can see a way of getting ashore."

"Good, go on," Andras said, surprised at the quick response

"If I'm right the order telling us we are interned was on Estonian official paper with some sort of coat of arms or Ministry title," Andras nodded, "I suggest we cut it out carefully and stick it on a large brown envelope, with blank papers in it, addressed to the Commander-in-Chief, Estonian Navy and marked 'urgent'. I put on my uniform to look as official as possible, and take the envelope ashore asking the sentry the way to the Fleet headquarters. I know it is in the building on the other side of the mobile crane because that is where the Captain was sent when he came ashore. I will speak to the sentry in an authoritative voice, in Russian, which I am sure he will understand. As I walk past the crane, which will be out of his view, I can duck into it over the back. It should work because Estonian sailors do not question authority, and they are scared to death of Russians. The fact that I am speaking Russian will make him think it is something to do with the internment. It is cold enough for me to wear a heavy coat so I can easily take wire cutters and a small metal saw to cut the cable."

Andras looked at Piotr and then at Artor with admiration.

"You've certainly given this some thought, well done," he told Artor whose shoulders visibly stiffened, "but we don't want the cable cut, that would give the game away and show that we have not accepted internment peaceably," he added thoughtfully.

"With respect, Sir," Artor interrupted, "I will not cut the cable straight through, I will saw through and snip away at different place and at different angles to show that it frayed through use and snapped under pressure." Andras and Piotr smiled and nodded.

"There is one snag," said Andras, "You may be out of sight of the sentry, but there are plenty of other people around, dockyard and military personnel, who might see you."

"We will have to stage a major diversion," Piotr joined in. "The crew will have to start a major row on the stern of the ship to attract attention. They will enjoy doing that and the Estonians will be so amazed they will all watch, and with a bit of luck, their backs will be to the mobile crane."

"Organise it," Andras said quickly. "They will start unloading again soon and we've only got six torpedoes left."

The small meeting broke up as Piotr went off to brief the crew and Andras and Artor began work on the envelope.

Many things had gone wrong for the *'Eagle'* since that awful day, 1 September, but fortune suddenly turned in their favour. Andras and Artor had just completed work on the envelope, and the latter had gone off to change into his uniform, when an excited Tomasz came into the Captain's cabin.

"I think we're having a real bit of luck," he told Andras, "a Russian destroyer has just entered harbour, and it looks as though it is going to tie up in the berth next but one to us - on the opposite side of the sub to the mobile crane. That means that everyone will be watching another foreign ship tying up and attention will be off us. We all know that whichever harbour you're in, anywhere in the world, everyone watches a ship entering harbour and tying up. If it's one of your own Navy you are hoping they make a mistake so you can have a good laugh. If it's a foreign ship you're watching to see what mess they make of it."

"Bloody hell," laughed Andras," how lucky is that! You are right, everyone will be watching. Go and tell Artor and help him get ready. Tell our chaps to join in and watch the Russians so that will attract attention. Better still, they can shout comments, rude or otherwise. No-one will understand them."

Tomasz went off to find Artor, laughing to himself. Life could be fun after all.

The fact that it was a cold day probably helped. The sentry on the *'Eagle's'* gangway was cold and bored and when Artor approached in his heavy coat, which caused some jealousy, he gave only a cursory look at the envelope and indicated with a careless arm movement where the headquarters where.

There was a steady background of noise, officials shouting orders and the sounds of capstans turning, as the Russian vessel began to manoeuvre carefully into position for tying up. It was going in stern first, to allow for a quick getaway, so that it was difficult and slower than usual. Tomasz was right, the interest in the ship was intense. Where normally two men would be waiting on the jetty to catch the mooring ropes, on this occasion there were four or five, or even more.

Artor, his heart beating rapidly, walked steadily towards the mobile crane noticing that, as predicted, everyone around had turned towards the Russian vessel, which was edging slowly into its berth. He quickly ducked behind some oil drums, which stood alongside the mobile crane, and was pleased to see that the crane's crew, which should be getting ready to re-start unloading the torpedoes, had moved away and were standing together with the rest of the watchers. He jumped quietly up into the back of the vehicle and found himself close to where the hoisting cable disappeared into the main cable roll.

Lying on his back, his 1.8 metre frame curled up to fit the space, he began, with hands he was surprised to find were trembling, snipping away at the wires that made up one of the three strands of the cable, moving the cutters slightly each time so that when the individual wires broke it was in a different place to the next one so that the end result would, hopefully, show that the cable had frayed. It went well and gradually a number of wires were broken and he began to worry whether he was being too successful and the cable would snap too soon. Eventually, after about twenty minutes, with the Russian ship still holding everyone's attention, he felt he had weakened the cable sufficiently. He looked around, removed any sign of his activities with his gloved hand, and slid backwards on to the ground. There was no-one around.

A smile and a nod was all he gave the sentry as he returned to the gangway and strode confidently back aboard the submarine. The smile was not returned.

It was nearly an hour later when the watching crowd dispersed and the mobile crane crew returned lethargically to work. The jib of the crane swung slowly round over the stern hatch of the 'Eagle' and lowered the lifting gear into the submarine where the loading team were waiting. It was another half hour before the lifting procedure began.

The tail of the torpedo had hardly appeared when there was a resounding snap followed by a huge bang accompanied by cries of anguish as the cable snapped and the torpedo dropped back into the submarine.

Artor, standing on the bridge, smiled broadly. He had got it right and there could be no mistake or wrong identification of who had done it.

"Got a problem?" Tomasz asked as he walked back towards the stern. An Estonian officer, standing nearby, said nothing, but indicated a breaking with his hands while making a snapping noise. Tomasz looked quizzically at him.

Eventually he walked from the crane to the submarine and shouted across; "Cable broke. We cannot replace it until tomorrow." Tomasz shrugged.

"That will teach the buggers," he thought, smiling to himself with satisfaction.

* * *

The successful disabling of the mobile crane was followed by further good fortune.

Kazik had been instructed to switch on the power to the gyro compass to give it time to warm up. In the control room an Estonian guard was watching carefully anything that happened, and showed great interest in the humming noise that started when the gyro was switched on.

Kazik noticed the interest and briskly fanned his face with his hand: "Additional air conditioning," he explained with a smile. "It is getting very warm in here." The Estonian nodded agreeably.

Andras looked around, contemplating the situation. The Estonian demand for the dismantling of the radio and engines had been temporarily stalled, and, of course, those working on the torpedoes now had no choice, to stop work. The plan had started well.

The discussion which followed was one in which the participants basked in self-satisfaction, but they were aware that there was still much to be done.

Everyone discussed their allotted tasks and a timetable was established. It was decided, after a long discussion, that the crew would turn in at around 2230 and would give the appearance of being sound asleep to put the sentries' minds at rest, that the crew had accepted their situation.

Piotr, Robert and Cazegorz, spent time working on the route out of harbour, instructing Jersey to make a smoke signal when instructed to.

Cazegorz recalled the route used when the *'Eagle'* was towed in. "Looking at it in reverse," he explained, "we have to pass the buoy in the centre of the harbour on our starboard side and then, almost immediately, turn to starboard and aim for the port side of the main entrance. That should see us clear, we must remember there is a shoal in the middle of the harbour, and I don't know how big it is. If we take too wide a berth we may run into shallow water near the harbour wall."

"That gives us a hell of a lot of confidence," said Piotr sourly. Jacek listened with cynical interest. Stefan was pretending he knew what they were talking about, but he really had not got a bloody clue.

Janwyn, looking every inch a devoted angler, sat on a bollard on the submarine wearing a heavy overcoat and an old hat, throwing the line in different directions as if to discover a shoal of fish. The watching guards smiled sympathetically at this idiotic behaviour. None of them could ever remember anyone catching a fish in this part of the harbour. The line Janwyn was using had knots tied every metre so that he could work out the depth roughly whenever the weighted line touched the bottom. He found the minimum depth to be in the region of seven metres, just enough for the *'Eagle'*.

He reported his findings to Andras who confirmed them with the planning group,, and that they would break out at midnight.

The crew turned in early as arranged and dropped off together in an amazing display of syncronised sleep.

The Estonians were not conscious of this and were, in fact,

extremely happy that the crew had accepted their situation and were not about to cause trouble.

Then the plan hit a snag.

At 2330 a senior Estonian officer, with an armed escort, arrived at the gangway and started to come aboard.

Tomasz, who was Duty Officer of the Watch, greeted them at the head of the gangway.

"Good evening," he said politely, smiling. "What can I do for you?"

"We are checking that all is well," said the Officer. "We have to come aboard and look around."

"That's not very considerate, I don't think I can agree," said Tomasz, still smiling. "Everyone is asleep. They have all had a very hard and emotional day, and they've got a bad day tomorrow as you continue your work and they go into internment. I think they deserve to be left to sleep, and this will not be possible if you are walking around."

The officer shook his head: "I am sure we will not keep them awake for long and then they can continue their recovery," he said, taking a step up the gangway.

Tomasz stepped in front of him: "If you insist I will have to wake the Captain and I am sure he will wish to check this immediately with your commanding officer, who is probably also asleep." Tomasz moved to turn away as if to get the Captain.

The Estonian hesitated, not wanting any trouble with authority, particularly his own who, he agreed, might also be asleep and would not welcome being woken up for a decision on such an unimportant matter.

"No," he said, after some thought, "we will leave it now, we will be back very early tomorrow morning."

"That is extremely good of you," said Tomasz. looking very respectful. "We will look forward to seeing you tomorrow."

The Estonian bowed politely, spoke to his men, and they moved away and did not notice Tomasz's heavy sigh of relief.

* * *

Tomasz went straight to report to Andras, who was lying on his bunk wide awake, to explain what had happened.

"There is too much activity out there," he suggested. "They are still very lively and would be suspicious if we started doing anything. I don't think a midnight escape is still on."

Andras looked thoughtful. "Get Piotr, Mucha and Ryzard, see what they think."

"Not a bloody chance," exclaimed Piotr when he learned the news. "We'd be spotted in seconds if we tried anything." Mucha and Ryzard agreed.

"We will delay it until 0200. We will still have time to get out while it is dark and they should all be asleep by then," Andras suggested to the agreement of the others. The news was swiftly passed among the 'sleeping' crew, most of whom welcomed the extra time to actually doze off or think.

Andras lay on his bunk going through the arrangements that had been made, to try and detect any omissions or weaknesses. When he had done that a dozen times and convinced himself that everything could, and probably would, go wrong he decided to think about something else, and immediately regretted it.

Although he tried, he could not avoid turning to something that he had been putting to the back of his mind since *'Eagle'* left Gdynia in a rush. It was something his fellow officers and the crew knew nothing about. A month before they left harbour his wife Alekzandra had told him that she thought she was pregnant, and the baby would be expected in March next year.

When he received the message it took his mind back to a time in July when they had left Warsaw, where they lived with his mother and father, to spend a few days together. It had been a wonderful time. They had never felt, or been, so close to each other. His first reaction was that the baby would make his family complete, and the rest of their lives together would be happy and fulfilled.

The memory was wonderful, the reality now was awful. Would he ever see the baby? Would it be a boy or a girl? Would he ever see his wife again? What would happen to them? The questions flooded through his mind. The pregnancy had been confirmed just before they sailed and he had hardly any time to talk to his wife, and enjoy confirmation of the news.

The appalling devastation the Germans were causing, since they crossed the border, would hardly be relaxed when they reached Warsaw. It seemed that there was no doubt that they would occupy all of Poland and that his son or daughter would be born in a country occupied by the enemy. He might never know what happened to them. He decided he did not want to think about it.

***

Tadeusz was having similar problems, although his involved his wife and mother, two people he loved dearly, had proved to be totally incompatible. In his mind he reviewed his visit home before his departure, even though he fought against it. On his last visit the atmosphere was cold and unforgiving. It seemed his mother, now nudging 70, had accused his wife of stealing money from her purse. Tadeusz knew his wife would never do such a thing, although when he told his mother, she accused him of siding with his wife, against a mother who had sacrificed her life and done everything for him. It was two days later, just before he was due to return to his ship, that his mother reported that she had found the money, she had forgotten she had put it in a drawer in her bedroom. That was all, there was no apology. Tadeusz had left them, holding on to the hope that the horror of the German occupation would eventually bring them together.

Jan lay on the deck, with his back against a torpedo, reflecting on the fate of his brothers, 19-year-old Josep and 15 year-old Mikolai. They were basically country boys with little experience of the world although Josep was at high school while Mikolai was still at elementary level. Both were expected to learn a trade and there was no doubt what trade they would learn, watchmaking. That the family tradition was now unlikely to be followed was highly likely, he thought. If the rumours he had heard were true Josep would either be conscripted into the army, or shot. It would depend largely on his attitude when approached by the Germans. Knowing Josep and his inherent dislike of authority the latter result was dangerously likely. Please God he would have more sense. Mikolai would be made use of in some way. But maybe the Germans would sweep through their village of Pezino on their drive to Stargard Szczecionski. The only point of interest in Pezino was the ruin of a 13th century monastery, and as they were busy creating their own ruins they might not be tempted to hang around an historic one. Jan's mind, like those of everyone on board was a twisted maze of uncertainty what was happening to those they loved.

* * *

At around 0130 the crew started stirring quietly, although none of them became obviously active. That would not happen until after the signal had been given by Andras to silence the three sentries, the one on the gangway, and those in the control room and on the bridge.

Those who were to silence the guards moved quietly into position. They looked a powerful trio that would stand no nonsense, and carry out their assignment effectively. The wiry frame and typical Slav features of Tadeusz contrasted with the small, but strong muscular figure of Gregorsz as they readied themselves for action.

The four men assigned to cut the mooring ropes met to check how they would get the signal and what to do.

One of the smallest members of the crew at 1.6 metres Dasay was argumentative, but not aggressively so. He simply enjoyed an argument and would take the opposite view to the person he was talking to just for the hell of it. Trouble was that few of his so-called 'adversaries' realised this, and they took him seriously. An uncontrolled bush of thick black hair crowned a round chubby face with soft brown eyes. Despite his size, no-one had any doubt that his enthusiasm would be enough to sever the hawser with one go.

Lukasz, the erstwhile priest, with his fair hair and honest and peaceful look, was quite capable of presenting a different picture, if aroused. He was anxious that he carried out orders to the letter and was keen to show his determination. If anyone was going to cut a hawser with one blow he was damn sure that it was going to be him.

One thing was certain, the speedy cutting of the hawsers at precisely the right moment, was going to be a competitive matter between Eryk and Marek. Eryk's approach was devil may care, one enthusiastic blow delivered with all the power available.

Marek's was more professional, carefully working out the right angle to hit the rope and how to ensure that the highest power was achieved, at exactly the right moment. Each man was sure he would win.

Ryzard, who had the important role of putting the dockyard in darkness, prepared with his usual care and precision. He was armed with a long handled wooden axe, sharpened, he said, to such a high degree that he could shave with it. He was sure it would do the job.

At 0155 Andras walked into the control room, smiling at the Estonian guard, and leaned over the chart table to look at the pieces of paper lying there. The guard, curious to see what he was looking at, went to look over his shoulder. The next moment Tadeusz had poked a revolver in his face, while putting his finger to his lips to indicate silence. The guard started to cry out, but it turned into a gurgle as Tadeusz punched him in the stomach, knocking all the wind out of him.

Tabbert, his pipe still firmly clamped in his mouth, crept quietly up to the bridge where the guard, half asleep, stirred when he heard a noise from the control room and was about to look down when a strong hand was clamped over his mouth almost suffocating him.

Gregorsz startled the gangway guard by walking purposefully along the gangway. The guard raised his rifle, but found it pushed up into his face and a hard punch on the point of his chin knocked him out cold.

At this point Ryzard, who had been waiting at the base of the conning tower, ran along the gangway on to the jetty, and raced the 60 yards to the substation. It was a cloudy night, so any moon there was was obscured and the dockyard was deserted. He smashed the lock of the gateway with one blow, and immediately spotted where the mains cable came out of the ground into the generator. He paused for a moment to concentrate, fixed his eye on the point he was going to strike, and with one mighty swing, using all his considerable strength, brought down the axe and plunged the dockyard into darkness. Throwing the axe away he sprinted back to the submarine as four energetic, enthusiastic sailors, with smaller axes and knives severed the mooring ropes. There was much shouting and aimless running around by those shocked by the sudden blackout as he re-boarded the submarine.

Jersey had already started the diesel engines and Cazegorz, with Andras on the bridge, began turning the wheel to point the submarine's bow towards the harbour entrance.

All had gone according to plan, and a feeling of optimistic satisfaction began to permeate through the crew when, suddenly, a machine gun opened fire spraying the conning tower with bullets.

"That's a bit bloody quick," said Andras crouching down with Piotr. "Someone must have been awake."

The submarine gathered speed heading for the mid-harbour buoy. With another, quicker than expected reaction, a second gun opened fire and a shell whistled over their heads landing shortly ahead on the port bow.

"They'll have to be bloody careful," grunted Andras, "or they'll hit one of their own ships."

"Or the Russian destroyer," Cazegorz added hopefully.

Cazegorz's instinctive reaction was to turn the wheel and carry the submarine closer to the buoy than he intended.

At the exact moment Andras spotted the lights of an Estonian patrol boat preparing to leave and give chase, there was a resounding bump and the *'Eagle'* shuddered to a dead stop throwing members of the crew off their feet. The submarine had hit the sand bank in the middle of the harbour, which they had been trying hard to miss. The accident, although critical and dangerous, gave Jacek great satisfaction. The thought that Cazegorz wasn't as clever as he thought he was, passed through Jacek's mind.

"Full ahead both, hard-a-port" shouted Andras down the voice pipe. Jersey reacted swiftly, the engines roared as blue smoke was ejected from the submarine hiding it from intending pursuers. As another shell fell even closer, the submarine shuddered again, but did not move. Another thrust of the engine. Another pregnant pause while 54 men held their breath. At last, a shudder, the submarine rolled gently and was free and jerked off the sand and back into deeper water.

The *'Eagle'* quickly gathered speed, half hidden by a cloud of blue smoke, and covered the rest of the distance to the harbour entrance in a matter of minutes.

More gunfire, this time including some of the bigger shore

batteries, hurled shells around the ship. At last *'Eagle'* was through and clear of the entrance and Andras immediately ordered Cazegorz to turn north towards the Gulf of Finland, knowing that pursuing ships would see them. As soon as she was well clear of the entrance, with shells still falling and more ships beginning to give chase he ordered "Dive, dive, dive!"

The bridge cleared quickly and the submarine sank slowly beneath the surface.

"Steer one seven five degrees," ordered Andras, turning the submarine almost 180 degrees, "so we head south along the coast of Estonia. They will expect us to go straight out into the Baltic and will be racing out looking for us," he explained.

"I bloody well hope so," Piotr laughed.

In the depths of the submarine a happy crew was cheering the success of the escape.

"We are free," shouted a voice, "now we can start sinking Germans."

"Yes," said a more pessimistic Piotr, "We have no charts, no navigational equipment, a partly damaged ship with no guns, nowhere to refuel or provision, and, they found, only six torpedoes. Where's the German fleet?"

The conversation that had broken out was suddenly stilled by a shout from the wireless room.

"Jesus Christ!" shouted Slawomir, appearing at the door of the wireless room "The bloody Russians have invaded Poland!"

The whole crew stopped dead in their tracks as if they had each been hit in the face. They stared disbelievingly towards the voice. They could not believe what they had heard. They had believed that things were beginning to get better, but now they were devastatingly worse. They looked at each other with furrowed brows.

It was not a self-centred concern, the news would not directly affect them for they would still be alone fighting the enemy. Their families at home, with the enemy approaching from all sides, and a notoriously unsympathetic enemy at that, would be in a terrifying position.

"The bastards," spat Marek, speaking for the whole crew. It was Sunday 17 September 1940.

* * *

SIX

The departure of the *'Eagle'* was marked by a 'goodbye and good luck' offering from the Estonians in the form of a bombardment of high explosive shells from the shore batteries. The combination of a small target and inaccurate gunnery meant that all the shells fell wide, short or too long.

The submarine moved to 'full speed ahead' as the harbour entrance fell behind. Andras looked astern with mixed feelings. To be free and back in action was exciting, but what lay ahead was disquieting.

A Captain in charge of a ship at sea can, in normal circumstances, expect to have technical apparatus, a chart showing the dangers, sea depths and coastal facts, a compass giving reliable readings, a regular weather forecast and a sextant with which to confirm his position, to help him with his decisions, and a home port for refueling and supplies.

Andras had none of these, so his basic feelings of uncertainty and insecurity were exacerbated. He felt like a blind man abandoned in a strange town full of traps, trying to lead a party of people dependant upon him to safety in a fog. So, it was with apprehension that he gave the order to submerge when he considered that the water might be deep enough. It was with half disguised relief when the submarine sank safely beneath the sea and to a safe depth without hitting anything. He immediately ordered a sharp turn to port to take them down the Estonian coast.

He had two reasons for this, he explained to his officers. He had already described his belief that the enemy would expect them to head straight out into the Baltic to get away as quickly as possible. His second motive was that he planned to drop the two Estonian prisoners, the guards, captured on board, on their home coast. The two of them had been released from the ropes that had held them during the escape and were now relaxing in the after torpedo compartment, not as prisoners, but more as guests, accompanied by three sailors as their hosts. They seemed happy and content, they were warm and comfortable and had been fed and had no understanding of the dangers that the *'Eagle'*, its crew and their guests faced.

The submarine rested quietly on the bottom with no sign of enemy activity. The avoidance ploy had obviously worked.

As dawn broke Andras decided it was worth a quick visit to the surface to check on their position in relation to the coastline. He also ordered a sounding to be taken to check on the depth of water. His decision was confirmed as wise when he saw to his horror that they were less than 100 metres from the rocky shoreline and that the water depth was less than 10 metres. He was grateful that they were not in the clear blue waters of the Mediterranean, where they would be clearly seen from the air, but in the murky waters of the Baltic and with the day cloudy and dull, the chances of being seen were small.

Andras had a mental general picture of the Baltic and a rough idea of where the major islands of Gotland and Bornholm, and the Gulfs of Bothnia, Finland and Riga where, but no detail. But the *'Eagle'* was fortunate in its crew in that they had a wide range of skills, talents and knowledge, so it was always possible to find the right man for the job.

In his current plight he was reminded that Robert, the

second engineer, knew the Baltic well and was something of a cartographer.

"You know the problem," Andras said to him, "what can you do to help?"

"Well I can draw a free-hand chart showing most of the danger areas and the main islands. Very broadly I know where the water is deep enough for us, and there's not much of it. I can use our Light List, the list of navigation lights in the Baltic which the Estonians did not remove. My imagination can do the rest," Robert replied confidently.

He also had a keen interest in all matters marine, and as the Baltic was the only sea of any interest to Poland, his knowledge was extensive.

Apart from Ryzard, Robert was probably the best informed member of the 'Eagle's' crew. His ambition had always been to follow his father, now dead, into the Polish Navy. To this ambition he added the desire to learn everything he could in as many areas as possible. Like Ryzard, he was fascinated by astronomy, but more as a tool for navigation than a scientific study.

He was also interested in people, what they were really like and how they reacted in various situations. As a result, he was the only member of the crew who understood that although Andras might seem to be in total control at all times, he had an under-lying lack of confidence which worried him considerably.

The strong silent type was the crew's view of him and he was a perfectionist. All this study had clearly had its effect for, although he was only 35 years old, his hair was thinning rapidly. He did not seem to realise this himself, for he had the habit of sweeping his hand through what was left of his hair as if he considered it an uncontrollable thick bush. Robert looked around at his audience, which included Andras and most of the other officers.

"Tallinn is roughly on latitude 59 degrees north and longitude 25 degrees east so we'll start there." He drew a wiggly line down the right hand side of the paper. "That is the Estonian coast," he explained. "There are two islands here, just north of the Gulf of Riga. I don't know their names so I will call this, the smaller one, the 'Isle of Piotr' and the other one, the 'Isle of Tomasz'."

"Why make my island the smaller one?" asked Piotr smiling.

"Because it is the most important one," Robert replied diplomatically. "I reckon we are parked just north of them at the moment so I suggest," he said, looking at Andras, "that we go between them through, let's call it the 'Andras Strait', on the surface during the night because the water will be very shallow. There's a navigation light on the western tip of 'Tomasz'. When we pass it we will be out into the Baltic proper and aiming for the Swedish coast. We should be well away from the Russian searchers. Then we can head south and start looking for Germans." He continued roughly mapping the coasts of Poland, Germany, Denmark and Sweden, putting in the Islands of Gotland and Bornholm.

"When we get near Gotland the water will be deeper as there's a trench almost all the way round the island. What we do then depends on what the news is," he added. looking questioningly at Andras.

"That is good," the Captain said appreciatively, "but we really do have to get some charts if we can. We might be able to stop a freighter and persuade them to give up their charts,. Tomasz," he turned to his torpedo officer, "get a small boarding party together and give them any arms we've got. You can lead them if we come across an unsuspecting freighter." Tomasz nodded.

"When it is dark we'll put up the aerial and find out what the news is and then decide what our next action will be."

The news, when it came, was surprising.

Andras and Piotr came out of the wireless room and walked to the after torpedo compartment where the two Estonians were still relaxing.

"You may be surprised to learn that you are both dead," he told them. "You have my deep sympathy. According to Russian radio we murdered you when we escaped and threw your bodies into Tallinn harbour. They have reported that both bodies have been recovered. However, my sympathy for you both is somewhat reduced by the fact that we have been sunk by a Russian destroyer shortly after we left the harbour. We were lost with all hands and there were no survivors. I think a few moments' silence on our own behalf would be appropriate," he told them solemnly

"Dead! The lying bastards," one of the guards, Jaan, exploded angrily. "They will have told my wife."

"I expect so," Andras replied. "What about you Helijor?" he asked the other guard.

"I'm not married, my mother will be devastated. We must go ashore and tell them as soon as possible. She is very old and the news might kill her."

"That brings me to another point," Andras said. "I am not going to put you ashore in Estonia as planned." The Estonians looked at each other in dismay. He had promised them he would give them the chance to get home.

"If I do and you show yourselves in your own country they will very quickly kill you. They could not allow you to suddenly turn up after all the lies they have told. Your presence would show them to be liars. They could not allow you to be seen after their reports. What I intend to do is to take you to Swedish territory and put you ashore there. You can tell the authorities what happened and prove you are alive, and they can tell your families. It is the only way."

After pausing for thought and looking at each other they realised the truth of his argument and nodded their understanding. When the babble of conversation, inspired by the news of their demise, had finally subsided, the crew settled down to their private thoughts. The air was deteriorating to its usual low level caused by the prolonged period of being submerged. It became hot and humid and the slightest movements caused sweating, clothing became uncomfortable and much of it was abandoned, and throats dry and sore. It was nothing unusual, they were used to it.

As always, at every opportunity their concern was with their families. They had them constantly in mind but at moments like this they remembered even the smallest details; things that to a stranger meant absolutely nothing, but to the men themselves were dear and important. A tone of voice, a way of speaking, the way they carried themselves, a passing facial expression, laughter, a habit of movement, they were the personal idiosyncrasies they remembered. Only a few men had photographs with them, fewer still had letters. These were not simply keepsakes they were treasures of the heart.

Most of the men had their last leave more than a year ago, at Christmas, and some had not seen their loved ones since then, but their images were as alive as if they had seen them yesterday.

One thing worried them above all others, the plight of their dear mothers. Would the lot of mothers never change, must their lives always be strewn with the crosses on graves of husbands, sons and brothers? They themselves would not even have crosses on their graves, the sea would take them as it had taken so many before, covering with its waters, new victims.

* * *

Tomasz, feeling as if his mind was floating in space, relived the dreadful day when he discovered that his great love, Alina had told him she was seeing someone else. He had known her since they were teenagers and they had been together ever since and there was never anyone else, for either him or for her, or so he thought.

He had a suspicion that something was wrong, but only slight doubts. She had not been as enthusiastic as usual when he talked about plans for the future and she was not always demonstrative. In love making her participation was not the same, although she seemed to enjoy it, it was a sexual enjoyment, not a loving partnership, two human beings becoming one. He thought at the time that it was probably a passing mood.

He was busy preparing for what might be war. The threat had been around for months and all conversations with friends, acquaintances, and people they met at dinner parties or socially, centred round the possible conflict. He knew that if and when it happened he would have to go to sea and thought maybe that the prospect of that was constantly on her mind. When the reality became known and he was told that there was someone else he was stunned. When he found out it was another sailor he realised that his profession, and the prospect of him going to war, was not the reason for the change in attitude. She simply did not want him anymore. She eventually confirmed this by telling him the other man's name and that, like him, he was a gunner in the Navy.

He clearly recalled the day he first met Marcin, at a naval club in Gdynia. He had asked, on the off chance, if he was a member and whether he was there. When it was pointed out that he was, in fact, drinking at the bar Tomasz, lost all control of himself, walked over and hit him. Without knowing who was punching him and why Marcin instinctively fought back and a vicious fight ensued. Marcin a younger and much stronger man, had beaten him badly. When Marcin found out who is assailant was, he decided to take no action and say nothing.

Tomasz knew it was wrong, that attacking a man of lower

rank was a punishable offence in the Navy and he could lose his commission and, in normal circumstances, be thrown out of the Navy. Although he didn't like it, and would not admit it, he was grateful for Marcin's silence. He too had kept quiet and the incident never became official.

Marcin had frozen when he walked aboard the *'Eagle'* and seen Tomasz. A hundred thoughts ran through his mind. Get the Captain to refuse to take the new Petty Officer, belt him again and take the consequences, ignore him totally. But he knew he could do none of these things, he would have to put up with it. It was a fact of life, he had no choice. Their lives might well depend on each other.

Since that first meeting there had only been minor clashes and they had largely obeyed the Captain's orders. Over time he had found that Marcin did his job efficiently. He had been brilliant during the escape and proved that he could be depended upon. But, he told himself he didn't like him as a man. Then, as he thought about it, he realised he did like him a bit. The man got on well with the crew and dealt with them fairly. But, he told himself, they didn't have to be friends.

Marcin lay on his bunk thinking about nothing in particular then he looked round and saw Tomasz, looking half asleep. What a shock it had been when he walked on board *'Eagle'* and saw the man he had fought over a woman and that man was his superior officer.

He had not known how to react when they met. It was the first time he could ever remember actually trembling with nerves. He was polite and had managed a faint 'Hello, Sir.' Marcin thought that Tomasz had turned out to be a very efficient officer and very fair. But he was sure he could never like him. Well, he thought on reflection that he did quite like and respect him. But they didn't have to be friends.

* * *

Kacek walked over to where Hreinski was sitting, his back up against a torpedo carrying around 500lb of explosive.

"Okay?" he asked him.

"Fine," said Hreinski.

"What about you know what?"

"Still there, not as bad as it was. It's not there all the time, goes away for a day or so, but comes back itching like hell."

"Not dropped off yet then?"

Hreinski smiled: "That's not funny. Couldn't happen could it?"

"Not likely, but you never know," Kacek replied enigmatically. "Anyway, I've got this for you," he handed Hreinski as small glass jar carrying some brown liquid. "Soak it in this for a while, every day for a few days and see what happens."

"What is it?" Hreinski asked suspiciously.

"I'm not sure, it's an old family recipe, secret, but it might work."

"How the hell can you produce an old family recipe secretly?"

"My father is a doctor." The answer seemed to nonplus Hreinski.

"I don't know, he said doubtfully, "could it do any harm?"

"The harm's already done. Let's see what happens," said Kacek as he moved away

* * *

While Hreinski was discussing the detrimental effect of his last sexual adventure, Jake was reliving his own, his first. He was 22 years old, had never been with a woman. He had been in the Navy, based at Gdynia, for three years, but the opportunity had never presented itself. He had listened to his shipmates returning from nights ashore with colourful tales about what they had done with women. Much of it, Jake thought, was the product of colourful imaginations, but some of it must be true. He was determined to find out what it was like for himself and eventually he achieved a situation where he thought he might.

He had been ashore at a drinking party where he met an attractive raven-haired beauty called Iwana. They had liked each other immediately and he had met her several times until it became clear to both of them that there was a desire for more intimacy.

It was a warm evening at the end of August when they met in the town's Long Market, a social centre and the scene of festivals of all kinds, and walked slowly down the Duga to the bank of the Radoni Canal. At a quiet spot, hidden by long grass and well away from the path, they lay down and kissed passionately. Jake became more and more certain that this was the time he was going to lose his virginity, but he had no idea how to go about it.

The reports he heard from his randy mates in the mess dealt in great detail with the sex act, but never spent time explaining the overtures and how they got round to actually doing it. It seemed to him that it was a question of trial and error. Try something and see what the reaction was. If what you did does not seem encouraging, stop and try something less suggestive and see what happens then.

He leaned over Iwana and kissed her gently, parting his lips slightly. She put her arms around him and parted hers. So far, so good. He placed his hand on her firm breast and moved it slightly. Okay. He moved his hand again gently stroking her. She pulled him closer. Taking a deep breath and going for broke her opened the three buttons on her blouse and slipped his hand inside.

Christ Almighty! She did not have a brassiere on and he touched warm flesh with nipples standing proud. He stroked them gently as he felt stirring in his trousers and slowly he became rock hard. What now? How the hell do you move to stage two?

Further planning was unnecessary, his questions were answered for him when she undid his trousers and pushed her hand inside grasping his pulsating member. Up to this point he had thought he was in charge, but he was soon disabused of this belief when she freed one hand, put it up her skirt, lifted her bottom and removed her knickers.

He knew what was about to happen, but in his ignorance he began to wonder whether she was a virgin. He had heard that the first time could be difficult and painful. She quickly pulled him on top of her and opened her legs, taking hold of his rigid penis again, guiding it towards her vagina. His worries were quickly allayed, she was not a virgin for as he felt himself touching her she thrust forward and felt the damp warmth of her body envelop him. He moved slightly and she groaned quietly. He lay there, frightened to move, for the whole of his being was concentrated between his legs and he felt something might happen too quickly if he even slightly shifted his body, and he would feel a fool. But she became more agitated, and began to groan, increasing the tempo steadily, until she suddenly shouted out deliriously. His own explosion followed and he felt himself pumping into her. It ended as quickly as it had begun and after a while he began to try and move away from her, she had wrapped her legs around him and refused to let him withdraw. He had no objections.

"That was marvellous," she whispered.

"Yes," he replied, feeling rather proud of himself.

They lay as they were for about ten minutes saying nothing, enjoying their physical union. Eventually Iwana began moving herself gently against him, and to his surprise he found his body stirring again. Before long he was as rigid as he had been earlier, and he resumed moving inside her and soon she was groaning and moaning again. A steady change of tempo until he was moving faster and uncontrollably, but this time several minutes passed before another unimaginable explosion for both of them and she was shouting so loud with ecstasy that he feared a passer-by might hear them. And then it was all over for a second time.

"You are very good," she said as at last they parted, her body jerking as he withdrew, as she re-adjusted her clothing.

"Thank you," he replied, trying to work out exactly what he had done to earn such an accolade. It had been mostly her doing. An hour ago he had been a virgin, and now he had done it twice. He congratulated himself. It would make a good story in the mess, he thought, and then, reconsidering, decided to say nothing. They would only make vulgar jokes about it.

Jake lay re-living the whole event for the umpteenth time. It had been much more memorable than any of his friends had described. He had immediately started planning another meeting with Iwana, then that bastard Hitler had intervened. He wondered whether he would ever see her again or have another opportunity with another girl. He lived for the day, or even the night. He had tried doing it to himself, as he knew the other men did when they could, but it was not the same, no warmth, no movement, no indescribable involvement of another person. Would he ever have a second chance?

* * *

The atmosphere in the submarine, with the breath of more than 50 men polluting the oxygen was becoming overpowering. The ever-present diesel fumes and the stink of decomposing food mixed with the sweat and stench of unclean bodies, affected the stomach; and lungs became dry, making breathing difficult. Condensation dripped from every cable and instrument. No-one talked for inhaling, just to stay alive, was difficult enough. There were times when several members of the crew realised that they could not stand any more, they couldn't breathe and their nerves were at breaking point. And as they realised that it was becoming impossible to continue living, and began to think what they could do to end it all, they began to realise they were still alive and they became aware that everyone else felt the same way, and no-way were they giving in. They were aware that each one of them was withstanding the anguish and fear because they did not want to be the first to crack.

* * *

At last relief came.

"Up periscope," ordered Andras, "prepare to surface." Suddenly there was movement as men quickly took up their posts, forgetting that only moments before, they were preparing to die.

Andras knelt down to meet the periscope's eyepiece as it rose and quickly, but steadily swung the periscope 360 degrees,

"Looks clear," he said to Piotr, indicating him to have a look and confirm his view.

Piotr took the periscope full circle: "Not a light, nor a sign of anything afloat."

"Surface," Andras ordered. The hissing of the compressed air displacing the water in the ballast tanks was a welcome noise followed, very quickly because the submarine had been in shallow water, with the sound of the conning tower hatch being opened. The Captain and two look outs leapt out.

"Open the blowers," was the next order and the remainder of the water in the tanks was expelled.

The noise of the diesels starting up broke the silence and a stream of air sucked in by the engines produced a welcome gust of fresh air.

"What's that funny smell?" a voice shouted.

"They call it fresh air, everyone should have some," came the reply, "it's good for you."

* * *

Andras and his two lookouts swept the horizon again with their binoculars. It was only when they had done this several times, to ensure that there was no danger, that they themselves could take a deep breath and savour the purity of the air. In normal circumstances they would have complained about the icy wind, which drove the temperature down sharply. But they were only too pleased to be able to breathe at all after the previous few hours, and the sweat of their bodies became cold and sent an acute chill through them.

The night was black with heavy cloud scudding over them and it was difficult to see where the sky ended and the horizon began.

Andras felt buoyant because for the first time it seemed that luck was on the side of the *'Eagle'*. The weather was in their favour because it would be difficult for any enemy surface ship to see their low profile in a sea that was choppy with a moderate swell. It occurred to Andras that some of the crew below may not be welcoming the slight pitching and roll of the submarine on the surface, and bouts of seasickness might increase their physical discomfort.

Using the voice pipe he summoned Robert to the bridge and told Piotr to work out a rota system to allow a few members of the crew a short time on deck.

"What do you know about these islands?" he asked Robert when he appeared, well wrapped up against the wind. Robert was very conscious of his own well-being and was always determined to remain as comfortable as possible at all times.

"Not a lot, "he replied shaking his head sadly and brushing his hair back. But as Robert always professed ignorance when a question was posed, and then came up with a fairly knowledgeable answer, Andras was not fooled.

"There are two biggish islands whose real names I cannot

remember and would not be able to pronounce if I could. The northern one 'Piotr' is the smallest and is pretty well devoted to fishing, so we ought to keep an eye open for small boats with no lights. The other one is mainly agricultural and is fairly low lying. The main seaport is on the southern coast so I don't expect there will be much activity this side, especially not with this weather. Our main problem is that what I have called, with all due respect Sir," he gave Andras a small bow, "the 'Andras Strait' may be difficult. The mouth is a bay about 8 kilometres across, but then it quickly narrows to maybe about a kilometre. It will be fairly shallow because its a sort of valley between the two islands. Then it broadens out to a bay, probably around 60 kilometres wide, and then, out into the Baltic. I am pretty sure that we would not be able to submerge in the narrow neck if the need arose, but once we are in the bay it will be okay."

"Thank you," said Andras, "I didn't think you would have much idea," he smiled. "It was very helpful," he added.

"Stay on the present course at half speed," he ordered Piotr who had come up to take over the Officer of the Watch duties. "We'll think about altering course in about an hour."

The morale of the crew had reached a new high, and as they took their turn on the deck even the cold failed to douse their spirits. That they were free again, and in charge of their own destiny, was a major boost. Most of them had put to the back of their minds, for the time being, the news that Russia had invaded Poland. There would be time to think about that when they were below and submerged.

The Estonians' morale had also risen for they began to see themselves as part of the crew of a successful ship. The suggestion that if they had been put ashore in their own country may have led to their deaths had come as a shock, but they understood the argument and were grateful that the Captain had even bothered to think about their well-being. Despite his difficult situation he had probably saved their lives.

The tension began to return however, when an hour later, the submarine turned to begin its hazardous voyage into the unknown through what had become accepted as the 'Andras Strait'.

Still on the surface, and at half speed, they headed into the total blackness that lay ahead. On either side the deeper shade of black of the land silhouette was only marginally visible. Heavy banks of black cloud raced quickly overhead. For the lookouts the situation was desperate. Few lights were visible, or were they lights, or simply spots before the eyes? It was impossible to concentrate on them for, if one tried, other lights appeared in the corner of the eye. They disappeared when you turned to look at them.

One of the lookouts, Jake, was on the point of shouting a warning that a light was visible when he thought he saw one just off the port bow. Or did he? When he looked for confirmation it was no longer visible. Or was it a light in a small boat that was temporarily hidden by the waves? Christ it was cold. His heavy overcoat, guaranteed to be windproof, was anything but. As the blustery wind caught him it infiltrated through his buttoned-down collar, chilling him to the core. Every now and then waves whipped up by the wind hit the submarine and sprayed water over the conning tower. It slowly seeped through his clothes, damping first his shirt and then his underwear. He had discovered long ago that it was impossible to make clothing watertight.

Why didn't we stay in Tallinn, he asked himself. It would have been warm and comfortable in a prisoner-of-war camp. But he knew the comfort of being berthed in Tallinn harbour would have soon disappeared in a prison camp. His day-dreaming was suddenly ended by a tap on the shoulder.

"My turn," said the muffled voice of Yarwin, hardly recognisable in his woollen helmet, scarf and sea coat. Jake's half hour duty on watch was over, he could now go below, get warm, have a hot drink, and sleep until his next shift. Within minutes of sorting himself out he had settled down.

Yarwin was alerted by what he thought was a dark object. In fact, there could be two. Could they be mines? No, they looked to be too big. He wished to God that Dasay, who had taken over on the starboard side, was being lumbered with this decision. He did not want the responsibility. But he had got it.

"Two objects 15 degrees on the port side," he announced, nervously committing himself.

"What do you think?" asked Mucha who had taken over as Officer of the Watch.

"Can't tell, Sir," replied Yarwin comforted by the fact that he was dealing with an officer he really knew. He would not get the bollocking he would get from any other officer if he was wrong.

"Could be a small fishing boat, about 200 yards away, no lights."

"Got it," replied Mucha. "You're right, looks like two small boats. No sign that they have seen us." In the dim light it was impossible to be sure, but there was no visible sign of life on either of them. "They're probably hiding below, keeping out of the weather. They would not expect anyone else to be around. Steady as the goes," he ordered the helmsman. Mucha seemed unworried.

"Well spotted," came the afterthought from Mucha which encouraged Yarwin who re-started his search as the two boats gradually fell astern and disappeared. There was no further cause for concern until the two island silhouettes gradually began to draw closer together as the Strait slowly narrowed.

Mucha, who was on his second shift on the bridge called Andras, warning him that they were about to pass through the narrowest part of the Strait.

"Any problems?" he asked Mucha.

"We passed a couple of fishing boats by about 200 metres,

there was no reaction from them so we are fairly sure they didn't see us, visibility isn't good, I don't think they were even looking. They must have done this trip a hundred times and would not be expecting to see anyone else."

"Good," Andras replied, studying the water ahead of them. The gap could now be seen clearly and no other shipping seemed to be around. The wind had risen and the water was becoming choppier. Andras aimed the submarine at the centre of the gap and maintained speed.

Robert, who had become the Captain's unofficial navigation adviser, joined him. A few lights became visible on the land on the starboard side.

"That will be Emmaste, a small fishing village. We should see the Emmaste navigation light shortly." No sooner had he said it than a flashing light could seen.

The land on the starboard side, 'Piotr Island' which had closed up quickly as they approached, began to fall away equally quickly indicating that it was a small peninsular. Shortly after the land on the port side began to draw away.

"The Baltic sea lies ahead, next stop Sweden," Robert announced. "So far, so good."

It was the fact that the wind, which had blown them through the 'Andras Strait', was from the East that was quietly worrying Andras. He had wanted to stay on the surface as long as possible, on the other hand, a storm now could be a blessing in disguise for it would also make it difficult for enemy ships to see them. An East wind could indicate rough weather.

"We need to head west for around 160 kilometres by which time we should be in the deep water north of Gotland Island. Then we can head south-west until we spot the Faroa or the Gotland light. We can drop the two Estonians somewhere between the two," Robert offered.

"Good thinking," Andras replied tersely, "then we can get on with the war."

* * *

The pendulum of life swings with the rhythmic inevitability of a metronome. A period of good fortune such as getting through the 'Andras Strait' without difficulty is, more often than not, followed by a problem.

'*Eagle's*' time on the surface had allowed telegraphist Jan to pick up news about Poland from the BBC, and other radio stations. It was not news to encourage the submarine's crew. Andras discussed the situation with Piotr and Tomasz, on whether to pass the news on to the men. They came to the conclusion that the officers had no right to keep the information from them. If they boasted about the boat's team spirit, they should act as a team and keep everyone informed.

He called those off duty to gather in the central area.

"We've been able to bring ourselves up to date with news from Poland. You don't need me to point out that it is not good, it is news you should know about. I am sure it will only make us more determined to cary on the war," he told his unsmiling audience

"Since the invasion on 1 September, German Stuka dive bombers have been attacking every town in Poland. Some 52 German divisions, 15 of them armoured, have sliced through the country. We, of course, had no armoured divisions with which to defend ourselves. Hundreds of civilians are reported to have been killed.

"The outpost at Westerplatte in Gdansk, the bombardment of which started the war, held out for a week. The Gdansk Post Office surrendered when it was doused in petrol and set alight. The surrounded naval base at Hel on the Mierzeja Helska peninsular is, as far as we know, still holding out. The Government evacuated Warsaw after four days due to heavy, continuous, bombing.

"The invasion by the Russians along the 1,600 kilometre frontier has exacerbated the situation, and tens of thousands of refugees are reported to be running around like hunted animals. The segregation of Jews has already begun and children are being taken from their families to special camps. Poles who show any resistance to the Germans are arrested and shot. Some have been hung from lamp posts as an example to others," Andras continued in a steady voice.

"I know it is going to be extremely difficult for all of you to take in what is happening, and the reasons for it. All I can suggest is that as far as possible you concentrate on what you have to do now. I intend, with your help, to do my best to strike back at the enemy in any way we can."

The meeting ended in silence, the men, their heads held low, their faces grim, walked away deep in thought. They all knew that Andras had painted a picture which would be with them forever.

* * *

Andras's ambition to quickly be able to get on with the war was granted with embarrassing speed.

"Ships on the starboard quarter," yelled a lookout excitedly. "Looks like a destroyer and several patrol boats."

"Dive, dive, dive!" snapped Andras as the first shell landed slightly ahead of the '*Eagle*'.

"The buggers must have been waiting round the island," he muttered as he followed the two lookouts, and Robert, down the conning tower hatch.

Suddenly the whole inside of the ship resounded with the noise of the klaxon as the diesel engines stopped and were replaced by the electric motors.

The sudden quietness was broken by the loud gushing sound of water bursting into the ballast tanks. Then this died down and finally ceased completely so that the ship became totally silent.

'Eagle' went into a steep dive.

The steady pitching and rolling of the boat on the surface disappeared completely and the submarine became steady even though it was only 10 metres down, periscope depth.

The order 'second under-water crew close up' came sharply and was repeated to ensure that those concerned in that particular watch move into position quickly.

The three Officer Cadets were assigned, in turn, to the duty of assisting the First Lieutenant in the control room who was in charge of the periscope. Close to him was the Coxswain with the Bosun acting as quartermaster. Petty Officer Marcin was on duty at the flooding valves; with a seaman messenger at the telephones and voice pipe.

The electric motors were now running, so the stokers who look after the diesels had been replaced by the electricians. In the forward torpedo compartment the team was also closed up ready to handle their deadly weapons as quickly as possible, although in *'Eagle's'* case it would have to be a damn good target if one of their precious weapons was to be used. The submarine settled down once again in its submerged role. The hydrophone operators, were sending reports of their signals every 15 minutes.

It did not take long before the patrol craft and anti-submarine boats were racing overhead letting off patterns of depth charges that pitched and tossed the *'Eagle'* in the boiling sea. More twisting and turning, shattered glass, gushing leaks and flickering lights. It was like being in a steel drum with someone banging on the lid with a sledge hammer. The silence that followed the explosions and the bursting of depth charges was like the door of a sound proof room suddenly being slammed shut and then, just as the brain has accepted to new conditions, it is thrown open to the clamour of a steel furnace.

The hydroplane operators, Guayne and Hreinski, white

faces against a dark background, crouched motionless over their control buttons. Even when they changed hydroplane settings there was no perceptible movement.

The silence continued. There were no sounds to report. Then a strange clicking noise, like the rhythmic ticking of a metronome. Ears are pricked to their highest sensitivity in an effort to determine whether the noise was getting closer or further away or whether the noises were louder, or weaker, or staying the same? What was their bearing? The order is given to turn hard a starboard to double back on themselves. Drops of condensation plip, plop, plip, plop as a deeper, loud cracking and snapping goes through the boat.

"It's only the woodwork settling," says the Captain calmly.

'Is it the interior structure weakening because it cannot stand the pounding?' was the question the crew asked themselves.

"Not a pleasant sound," the captain remarked with massive understatement. More noises are reported, they are getting fainter. As they seemed to be drawing further away Andras decided to go up and have a look.

"Up periscope," the order is followed by the hum of the motor.

"Damn and blast," shouts the Captain. "Down periscope, go to 15 metres. There's a bloody patrol boat, stationery, waiting to trap us"

Once again the ear shattering noise as a depth charge attack is repeated, the continuous vibrations nerve-racking. But any member of the crew with a tendency towards panic is immediately calmed by the imperturbability of the Captain.

For two hours the frantic German vessels threw depth charge after depth charge into the agitated waters. Andras, trying to anticipate how the patrol vessels would react, alters course several times and then orders: "Stop engines, keep silent."

* * *

Three weeks of tension, for one reason or another, and their determination to carry on the war against the Germans, had hardened most of the crew of the *'Eagle'* and as a result most of them sat quietly at their posts seeming to ignore the world around them.

Henerey continued to his personal battle against claustrophobia by never taking his eyes off the depth dials, which he controlled, concentrating on every movement and by telling himself what every change meant, and what the next movement would be, up or down. He ran his own personal mental competition keeping the total in his memory, and was quite proud of the fact when the number of correct guesses outnumbered the failures. Sod doing what Tadeusz had suggested about thinking about wide open spaces: Even if I did they would only be full of bloody Germans," he thought.

Lukasz tried a mental exercise, running through the books of the Bible, trying to recall them in the correct order. Did Leviticus come before Numbers, or was it the other way round? He was okay with Matthew, Mark, Luke and John in the New Testament, Galatians, Ephesians and Philippians left him cold. He could not even spell them. When he checked with his dog-eared bible later, always kept out of the sight of the crew, he was disappointed with his failure to get many correct in the Old Testament and he was a little better with the New.

Guayne spent his time worrying about what had happened to his beloved dog. Who had his friend turned to when Guayne left to go to sea. It was, he thought, most likely that his 18-year-old girl friend Gizela, would look after the dog simply because it was the nearest she could get to him during his absence.

True to form Jake was mentally laying bets on the time

between explosions. His favourite bet was two to one against the next explosion being under five minutes. He put a mental stake on each bet, and true to form he was losing money fast.

Tadeus walked round quietly talking to the crew, making sure they were handling the situation, and cracking jokes if he thought it would help.

In the after torpedo compartment the situation was very different. The two Estonians were petrified. Ashen faced and stiff as broomsticks they both showed obvious signs of their fear. Jaan's trousers were soaking wet at the front while Helijor was having great difficulty sitting, his trousers obviously full. It was very clear that they were having trouble at both ends for they both looked as though they were going to be sick.

Mucha, the gunnery officer, who spoke Russian well, tried to comfort them and explain that they were quite safe. He thought about reminding them that they had their backs against a substantial amount of explosive, but decided against it. They might have died of fright.

"I did not think it would help," he told his colleagues

*   *   *

"I still do not know what happens when we die," said Jake, breaking the silence.

"Not that again," grumbled Dasay impatiently.

"It's still a problem," Jake insisted.

"What is?" asked Eryk, who had not taken part in the original debate, his eyes flashing around the assembly.

"The silly sod is worried that when he dies he won't know unless someone tells him, and he wants to know who that will be," explained Dasay.

"Well it won't matter, said Eryk, "he won't be there.

"What do you mean?" asked a mystified Jake, "I won't be there."

"Well you won't. You'll be gone."

"What do you mean - gone? Gone where?"

"Dead, Gone. No longer around. Snuffed it. When you die that's it. Finished. You no longer exist. That's it. Kaput," said Eryk with conviction.

"Not necessarily," Marek interrupted. "The body is kaput, of no further use, like an old coat, but the soul lingers on."

"Arse hole?" asked Dasay. His comment was accompanied by groans.

Marek ignored the crack, held Dasay with a steady gaze full of scorn. "If you believe that there is an after-life there has to be a change-over system. Your conscience will still exist, so it has to be guided in the right direction otherwise it is in a vacuum."

"Too much for me" Eryk grunted. "I would rather that be it. No more problems."

"If you believe what is in the bible then you believe in an after life," Lukasz offered.

Everyone remembered that if the war hadn't stopped him he would have trained to become a priest. "It tells you of paradise to come."

"Well, death can't be that bad," said Waldemar with assurance.

"How do you know that?" asked Eryk, surprised.

"It's obvious, everyone does it sooner or later," Waldemar laughed, "so it must be okay."

"Very bloody funny," snapped Eryk

Dasay snorted angrily. "What a load of crap. If you are good on earth you will be rewarded by going to a land of milk and honey when you die. It's rubbish. When you are a child you are told that God is everywhere looking after you. And most of us believed it. Look at Poland today and the hell they are going through. Where is He?"

The emotion raised by that remark ended the conversation.

* * *

The atmosphere became subdued as the crew got down to cleaning up the resultant mess as best they could, their minds began to re-absorb the news from Poland.

The visions of thousands of civilians being killed by ruthless dive bombing, of tens and thousands running around panic stricken, searching for safety, after the invasion by the Russians, in a country where there was no such thing, flashed through the minds.

It was impossible to equate people they knew and loved being subjected to the appalling visions conjured up by the news. Poland was a peaceful, beautiful land in which friendly, kindly people went about their daily lives of work, play, eating and drinking, socialising, love and sex, without crime and evil thoughts.

How could it have become a hell on earth? Was anywhere unaffected? Had anyone escaped the horror? While the crew of the *'Eagle'*, the warriors, had so far been playing at war, at home the ones they loved, unarmed, were fighting for their lives against a vicious, heavily armed enemy with no mercy.

They thought about their homeland. A country of open fertile land, woods and unspoilt lakes, of sandy plains, broad primeval forests and hills formed by glaciers millions of year ago. Of sublime coasts in the north, majestic mountains in the south, and the rolling countryside in between. A land of magnificent medieval architecture which had stood the test of time, until now. A land with a turbulent history, subject to attacks from other European countries, but nothing as bad, never as bad, as what was happening now.

* * *

It had been quiet for over an hour, with no noises being picked up by the hydrophones, before Andras decided to take another look round. It was dark by now and the electric batteries desperately needed re-charging. As the submarine rose to periscope depth it took on a gently rolling and pitching movement which meant that the weather on the surface was deteriorating.

Andras took a quick look round the horizon as the periscope broke the surface. The horizon was clear, but the waves were agitated and white topped. A second, slower, circuit with the night periscope confirmed that it was safe to surface, that no patrol boats were silently lurking to trap them again.

As the conning tower hatch was opened a huge wave deposited half its contents down the hatch soaking the Captain and his two lookouts, Hreinski and Waldemar to the skin guaranteeing them an uncomfortable watch.

A steady gale blowing from the east, which was a welcome acceleration to *'Eagle's'* surface progress, was not wholly acceptable to the crew below. Sea sickness was now the great worry for many of them. Those who, shortly before, had feared death by explosion and drowning, were now beginning to welcome it as an escape from the way they were feeling.

Another concentrated study of the surrounding sea convinced Andras that all was clear. He turned to Andrzej who was now Officer of the Watch. "Next stop Gotland," he suggested.

* * *

The *'Eagle'* plunged its bow into the churning water and each time it did it threw up a huge wave which enveloped the boat, sending gallons of water over the conning tower and into the submarine. Andrzej and the two lookouts struggled to maintain their feet and their vigilance, but found it was almost impossible.

A rough sea can inundate the boat throwing gallons of water down the conning tower and into the boat soaking everything and making the hot atmosphere damp and humid. Below, the crew and contents, including food are thrown around relentlessly as the deck convulses with the pitching and tossing and rolling. Violent change in weather made itself felt in the interior of the hull.

Habit accustoms the men to some immunity from so-called sea-sickness, it is the physical exhaustion coming from the constant effort to keep upright that is the crux of the matter. The bows of a submarine behave eccentrically, describing circles and figures of eight as well as diagrams which have no relation to time and space.

One solution is to climb into your bunk and sleep, as those off duty always do. Only the men on watch looking after the security of the vessel are alert. All the lights in the crew's space are switched off. Nothing but the swish of passing waves joins the heavy breathing of the sleepers and the discrete sound of music from the loud speakers around the torpedo tubes. The music, Andras thought, would have a calming effect.

At midnight all is bustle when the watch changes. Middle watchmen are shaken awake without ceremony and hurry to relieve their friends. The men from the bridge come down wet and cold, and go straight to the hot tea awaiting them. Each man takes out his loaf of bread or any other stored item of food and settles to a meal. Wet clothes are removed and shaken, the Coxswain gives tot of rum to men coming off duty.

Slowly those below find that the weather seems to be changing for the better. It may be that the sub is steering a course adjusted to the length of the swell, or that the crew is getting more accustomed to the roll. The precipitous, unbridled pitching and rolling turns into a slow rhythmic and monotonous motion.

Engineer Jersey became concerned by the amount of water slopping about, particularly conscious of the danger of it affecting the batteries and causing deadly chlorine gas. He collected a small team to help clear out water. In normal conditions this would be pumped out, but when the pumps cannot be used, when, for example, enemy vessels above are using detectors to find the sub or, because of a storm, it becomes overwhelming. The water has to be moved from the stern to the bow in order to keep the submarine's balance. When the air is fresh this is easy, but when the submarine has been submerged for a long time, the atmosphere thickens for, of course, air circulators are also switched off to avoid detection.

The crew, now feeling immune to the difficulties and discomfort, began passing buckets from forward to aft in a steady chain, fighting to keep their balance, fighting their feelings of sickness and fighting against the water which continues to fall on them. Gradually the water comes under control although the submarine continues its unsteady progress, and Jersey begins to feel that another small victory had been achieved.

* * *

The two Estonians, Jaan and Helijor, who had become calmer when the attacks ceased and who were now suffering from the seasickness of an intensity which a landlubber could never conceive, had hardly moved since they left Tallinn and were still in the after torpedo compartment. At first they had been fascinated watching the activity going on around them; then they had become bored as the submarine sat on the seabed. This had changed to concern as the atmosphere deteriorated and it became difficult to breath, then totally panic stricken as the '*Eagle*' was attacked. They had been relieved when told that they were not being put ashore in Estonia because they would most likely be killed, then grateful to learn they were being put ashore in Sweden. Now their stomachs were totally out of control and they began to wonder whether being put ashore in Estonia might not have been better.

"Is everything okay now?" asked Andras approaching them with a friendly smile. They both nodded.

"We are now on our way to the island of Gotland which belongs to Sweden and we are going to put you ashore there. We will give you a boat, food and water and money to pay your way back to Estonia. You can go back once the Swedes have revealed that you are still alive, so you will be safe when you get home," Andras explained, expecting overwhelming gratitude from the two men. But neither responded immediately.

"No," said Jaan eventually, in Russian. "We do not want to go back. We want to stay with you. You have been very kind."

"That is not possible," said Andras. "You are not submariners and we only have room for trained men, we cannot carry passengers. During the last attack you were both terrified and had to be looked after by a member of the crew;. This weather must have made it worse for you. We do not have time to look after you and there will be more bad weather, some much worse, and more attacks. I would have thought you would not want to suffer more. We will put you ashore in Gotland, probably tomorrow."

"We want to stay. We will work," Helijor joined in. "We do not want to go back. We will not go ashore."

"You will do exactly as you are told," snapped Andras. "You are not guests on board, you are our prisoners, as we were once yours," he almost snarled as he walked away.

"Keep an eye on them," he ordered.

* * *

Slowly the wind died down, the sea dropped to an acceptable level and the horizon became clear and visible. The early light of dawn warned of the coming day. Andras was anxious to get as close as possible to Gotland, land the Estonians, get away quickly and continue the journey submerged.

Gotland is the largest island in the Baltic and has belonged to Sweden since 1645, after being conquered and occupied by the Dames for 300 years. Its only major town, and seaport, is Visby on the western coast. Andras aimed to drop the Estonians near a group of islands on the northeast corner where there would be less shipping.

Andras dropped the *'Eagle'* down to half speed, and then slow, and began to edge the boat between the islands close to the mainland.

"We are going to drop you here. There's a small village, Robert thinks its called Slite, just over there," he explained pointing to his left. He produced a piece of paper which he handed to Jaan. "Piotr has produced this in Swedish. It explains who you are, why you have been dropped here and that the Russians had claimed we had murdered you. Keep it and show it to anyone in authority. Try and make your way across to Visby, it's not far." He gave Jaan another package.

"Here is some food and water and money to pay your fare back home. But make sure that the Swedes announce the fact publicly that you were not killed, but were looked after by us. That is important and makes sure the Russians will not be able to kill you when you get back. You can also remind people that we were not sunk."

Jaan who, with Helijor, had got over the fact that he could not stay aboard, looked at Andras gratefully. "You have been very kind. You could have killed us, but you didn't and you could have put us ashore in Estonia, you thought of our safety. All your men have been kind and helpful. We wish you luck in the future." They shook hands.

The *'Eagle'*'s' motor boat had been prepared and was lying alongside. The Estonians clambered aboard with difficulty. "Aim for that headland," Andras told them, pointing. "Best of luck." The boat started and began to draw away. The Estonians, almost tearful, stood up and waved as they slowly disappeared into the distance.

"Back to the war," said Andras.

* * *

SEVEN

The past three weeks had been a period of continuous tension. The crew had faced almost every terror that can be visited upon a submarine, with the addition of capture and escape. Long periods of life under water in uncomfortable conditions had been punctuated by depth charge attacks and foul weather. Everyone had had to be alert for 24 hours a day, every day.

Now, as Andras had said, having put the Estonians ashore they could get back to fighting the war. It proved to be an anticlimax. Their prize targets were enemy warships, but for several days they saw no sign of them, and life aboard fell into a routine dictated by the sun, submerged by day, on the surface at night, Half the crew on duty while the other half rested.

There is no such thing as 'Reveille' on a submarine, and that is of some relief to mariners. Whenever they had time they either slept, talked, played cards or did what else interested them. When duty called, whatever the time of day or night, they had to be on full alert. Speed and alertness were the first consideration, no matter what the rank of the individual.

A typical day saw the Officer of the Watch and an Officer Cadet on the bridge with two crewmen as lookouts, continually searching the horizon for any presence such as smoke from a distant ship, the shadow of a ship, a periscope with its small white bow wave, aircraft, or a mine.

Anything unusual had to be reported it to the officer on the bridge. Cazegorz, the Coxswain or his deputy, continually manned the conning tower and two or three stokers were always on duty in the engine room.

In the crew spaces the cooks were preparing meals. The only ones eating were the ones about to go on watch, thus avoiding unnecessary overcrowding. For those off duty they could have the luxury of breakfast in bed, simply by stretching out an arm and grabbing the food off the nearby table.

At this time the prevailing spirit was one of harmony in spite of the fact that as many as twenty men were cooped up in the tiny crew space. Those on the '*Eagle*' were the usual mixture of types and characters found on any warship, except that there were none of the extremes. The short-tempered, egotistical, self-opinionated bigoted and selfish had no place among the crew. Each man was an expert in his own area, some in two, and all of them had a basic knowledge of other areas. Tempers ranged from the quick and impatient to the jovial and frivolous, but they were all well controlled.

Signalmen off duty talked about what they had seen, what the weather was like, where the course was likely to take them, and discussions on arrival time at sector or destination.

Conversations included anything which meant dealing a blow to the enemy, of firing a torpedo and what kind of vessel would be a popular target. Names of the largest German ships were mentioned even though most of them were trapped in harbour, although they were not aware of that.

Of course not all conversations and discussions were of a high intellectual nature and of far reaching importance.

Andrzej, for example, spent much of the quiet period walking round ensuring that everything was in its right place, the habit that had gained him 'Toucher' nickname. Rapid signals would be flashed round the submarine informing those interested that 'Toucher' was on the way. He was a great asset to Jake, who took great delight in laying bets with anyone interested in what the Lieutenant would touch first when he entered the compartment. The peace and calm that had descended on the submarine and its crew provided the ideal atmosphere to encourage Jake to play his favourite game.

The cry 'Toucher's coming" given by Waldemar warned those in the forward torpedo compartment playing cards that an inspection was imminent.

"Bet you half a day's pay that he will touch the port torpedo and pat it like a mother with a baby," Jake offered quickly.

"No," Guayne challenged, "it will be the fan as he walks in, he will check that it's working."

"I say he will touch the locker door," Waldemar offered, while Hrienski suggested the table which was being used for a card game. A comedian from the back, left with little choice, suggested he would touch the deck first with his foot. Although he was shouted down Jake did asked him "left or right foot?"

The innocent Andrzej, a tall man with aquiline features and a friendly manner, walked into the compartment with a cheery greeting stopped, looked at the card table and asked: "What's the game?"

"Poker, Sir," Jake told him. "Would you like to join in?

Andrzej shook his head. "You would be too sharp for me," he said, leaning against the port torpedo.

Much to their surprise he turned quickly; called "Best of luck to all of you" and walked out.

"He's frightened to stay in case we talk him into a game and he loses," suggested Dasay.

"I win,"cried Jake excitedly," he touched the port torpedo."

"No, you did not," countered, Waldemar. "He did not touch it, he leaned on it."

"Leaning is touching," claimed Jake.

"Leaning is leaning. You have to use your hand to touch and he did not touch anything."

"The bet is off," Waldemar insisted

"He's right," Guayne confirmed. "If I leant on you, you would say, do not lean on me, you would not say don't touch me." Everyone nodded in agreement.

Jake looked round in despair, realized he was in the minority: "Sod the lot of you," he snapped.

"That means you owe us all half a day's pay," Waldemar suggested.

"I bloody don't, the bet is invalid as you say he did not touch anything, "Jake claimed.

"I don't have to pay a bloody penny. Let's play cards."

* * *

Everyone knew that the long period of inactivity would not continue, and within hours apprehension was arising once again. But it was a feeling of excitement and, for the first time, to be welcomed for it seemed that the chance of action was at last coming.

The first sign was recognised by the crew the next day. Although it seemed quiet on the surface the submarine had remained submerged for some hours even though it was late evening and dark. Rumour had it that there were trawlers still in their sector and they began to expect another long period of misery and discomfort. But before long the First

Lieutenant, Piotr, increased anticipation by explaining that the Captain had reason to believe that the German battleship *'Gneisenau'* was reported to be passing through their sector.

Enthusiasm rippled through the submarine. A 39,000 ton German battlecruiser with nine 280mm guns! One of the newest and best! What a target! What a way to get revenge after all that has happened! Even if they could not sink it, to severely damage it would be a triumph.

The only voice of caution was the Chief Yeoman Zygmont,

an experienced submariner, who could not help envisaging what the response would be.

"The escort of a major capital ship will be bloody formidable," he warned, "and if we were to be even spotted they would go berserk. If we hit it our world would explode."

But others, particularly Tomasz, were anxious to at least have a go and to hell with the outcome. He knew that he had only six torpedoes left, but they were useless just waiting to be loaded and used. This was a heaven-sent opportunity to use them and it must not be missed.

The submarine stayed at periscope depth with Andras continually sweeping the horizon searching for the enemy ships, knowing instinctively that everyone in or near the control room was watching him and anxiously waiting for news.

"I can't see any sign of the bastard," he announced eventually. "There are two destroyers and plenty of patrol boats and trawlers, but not the real target. I'm beginning to think that the reports were rubbish."

"Two destroyers are not much of an escort for a ship of the importance of *'Gneisenau'* " Piotr pointed out. "It would have at least one cruiser with it."

"Down periscope," Andras ordered. "It's nearly dawn. Let's wait until daylight and see what we can find then." Those in the control room relaxed and the mood gradually swept through the rest of the submarine.

The *'Eagle'* headed slowly north-east towards the island of Bornholm. Andras calculated that if the *'Gneisenau'* was in the Baltic it would not go far away from the naval base at Kiel and the canal and, anyway, it would have to return there eventually. He found it difficult to convince himself that the warship was there at all. What would it be doing in the Baltic? Only, perhaps, on a training exercise.

An hour passed before Andras ordered a return to periscope depth and began another search.

"Still no sign of it, but the two destroyers, some patrol boats and a pack of trawlers are around. I am surprised there are so many."

"They could still be looking for us," Piotr offered. "They will know we are still in the Baltic because if we had gone into a neutral port they would have heard about it and........"

The conversation was interrupted by the telegraphist Jan coming out of the wireless room, his face ashen white. He handed a piece of paper to Andras. A look of horror came over the Captain's face as the blood seemed to drain out of it.

"It has just been broadcast by the BBC that Warsaw has capitulated. It has been destroyed by the Nazis. Poland has surrendered to both the Germans and the Russians."

Andras dropped his hands to his side and looked into space as those around him stood stunned. No-one said a word.

For a moment it seemed that the end of the world had come. The words the Captain had used went through the minds of the stunned crew, there was a sense of unreality about them - Poland had surrendered, it was like an announcement that was of no immediate interest, just a statement of fact. Then the thought flashed through their minds that this meant the war was over. No more fighting, no more looking for German warships. Then the question, did this mean us? What would we do? Where would we go? Would we be prisoners of war? Then, a flash of realisation: we will still be at war, fighting on until the end. We have no choice, we still have to avenge what has been done to our familes, to those we love This was followed by the ironic conclusion, satisfaction that they would still have an aim in life.

After several minutes of total silence Andras turned to those around him, looking stern and determined and put the situation into perspective.

"This means that we really are totally alone. We cannot expect help from anyone or anywhere. We now have only one purpose in life and that is to wreak as much damage to what is still our enemy as we can. We must seek them out and strike a blow for Poland and our families. Nothing else matters."

In the back of his mind his thoughts were much different. How the bloody hell can we go on without any help, he asked himself. It was that moment that confirmed and strengthened the Captain and his crew as one.

The common joys and cares, the common ideas, aims and task, and the dangers and hardships were shared alike, and united the men even closer with their Captain. Their affinity became something special bringing them even closer together, into that sort of relationship normally felt only at home, or in the circle of those who are nearest and dearest.

* * *

The emotional moment passed as Andras returned to the business in hand, checking what was happening on the surface.

"There are no signs of a battleship, but what is interesting is that the two destroyers are in line abreast off our port bow, about two miles away," he said to Piotr and Tomasz who were by his side. "One is slightly ahead of the other and they are going to cross our bows eventually. If we can fire two torpedoes at them, as they cross we will almost certainly hit one of them, and with a bit of luck we could hit them both." He paused as his two companions smiled broadly.

"Let's go for it," Tomasz said grinning with pleasure as Andras nodded, and ordered his team, Kazik, Artor, Eryk and Marek to their posts.

"Flood numbers one and two tubes."

The now familiar chain of events was set in motion. The faint noise of water rushing into the torpedo tubes, the almost imperceptible dipping of the bows as the water filled them, the gradual increase in tension as the moment of action drew near.

"Tubes flooded," came the report to the conning tower as a fresh cluster of red lights flash on the control board.

A dull silence prevailed inside the boat. Only the monotonous lapping of the waves as the engines were stopped, and the quick breathing of the crew could be heard.

"Standby" said the Captain, checking for the last time, the accuracy of his aim. His eyes were straining at the periscope as he watched the two enemy ships, broadside on, one slightly ahead of the other, begin to cross the bows of the submarine.

"Fire one, fire two," he delivers the short order quietly. A slight recoil is felt throughout the whole boat.

The routine, usually well practiced, but now a novelty on the *'Eagle'* through lack of opportunity - loading the torpedoes, diving, aiming, pressing the firing, button to send an electric current through the electromagnets which, in turn, opened the pressure air bottle and send the torpedo on its way.

A small cloud of vapour, due to the compressed air forcing the water through certain joints in the form of a fine spray, appeared round the after part and rear door of the tube. Now it was a question of waiting.

Suddenly there was a severe shock, shaking the submarine viciously. A bomb from an aircraft had dropped close by.

"Take her to 35 metres." the Captain ordered.

"I hope we have got 35 metres," muttered a hopeful Piotr.

"Just after we fired the torpedoes a patrolling aircraft must have spotted the torpedoes leaving traces on the surface and they could possibly see the shape of the submarine so they let go their bombs, luckily bombs and not depth charges. They must have exploded on the surface just above the submarine."

"Did we hit anything?" Tomaz asked, his question full of doubt.

"I didn't see, but there were two explosions so we must have hit something. "We'll go back up in a minute and have a look," answered Andras.

Another shattering blow shook the submarine, throwing the crew into untidy heaps of humanity. Water dripped from small leaks in valves.

The Captain ordered: "Hard-a-port." Speed is forcing the boat down at a steeper angle than usual, but the Captains still ordered "All hands forward."

The cavalcade of men scrambled through the compartment. Everything began to slide, forcing desperate looks from the tumbling men. Leather jackets and binoculars hanging on either side of the hatch stood out at strange angles from the bulkheads.

Andras rested one thigh on the chart desk, his bent back and the dim white of his cap over the upturned collar and of his fur jacket giving the men a comforting silhouette of their Captain.

Piotr's eyes are almost completely closed, slits carved in wood with a sharp chisel. He sucked his lips between his teeth. His right hand held fast the housing of the sky periscope. Mucha, the Officer of the Watch, straightened up. His fists were knotted and he bared his clenched teeth like an ape. It is obvious he wants desperately to shout, but he could only swallow. No-one moved. Marek, in. the control-room, stood motionless, one hand on the ladder, head turned to face the depth manometer. The two hydroplane operators, Hreinski and Waldemar looked like stiff dummies in rubber suits, sou'westers gleaming with moisture. The pale eye of the manometer pointed to steady. Dasay, dazed and frightened, suddenly registered the fact that the hydroplane operators are still wearing their sou'westers and thinks how stupid they look.

Another shattering blow sent the crew sprawling again. There is the crash of breaking instrument glass.

Marek pulled himself upright, automatically staggered forward a couple of steps, jostled against someone, collided with a hard corner and collapsed into the hatch frame.

This is it he thought, I must not let go. He pressed his left shoulder hard against a metal frame of the hatch and made himself as heavy as he could. He seized with both hands, the pipe that ran under his thighs.

Blow after blow hit the submarine as if the sea was a mass of huge powder kegs being set off in quick succession. Outside nothing, but rearing, gurgling, rumbling. Undersea whirlpools seized the boat, tossing it violently this way and that. Most of the crew managed to jam themselves into a position which would withstand the blows hitting the submarine

Jersey staggered into the control room. His face was chalk white, beads of sweat gleamed like glycerine on his forehead. He hung on first with his left hand, then with his right.

Four detonations in quick succession became almost a single blow.

"Astern," the Captain pointed out quietly, "most of the explosions are astern." His remarks are meant to point out that the depth charges are falling behind and of little danger.

Another single detonation - not close, but the echo was remarkably long. The bubbling and roaring seemed never-ending.

Despite the urgency Andras gave no new orders to the helmsman. He was postponing any change in course until the last moment so that the attacker that was speeding after the boat would not have time to copy his manoeuvre.

"They really don't seem to like us," said Eryk to Marek, trying to lighten the atmosphere and show he was not frightened.

"I don't know what makes you say that," Marek replied, getting the point. "They don't even know us."

Another gigantic sledgehammer hit the boat. At almost the same instant Andras ordered the speed increased, but as soon as the tumult outside ebbed away he had the motors reduced to slow.

Another three, four blows so violent that the deck plates clattered. Everyone felt the detonations right down to their stomachs. Water seemed to be dripping from every joint, but few noticed it because they were already soaked to their skin by the sweat of fear.

Andras hadn't budged an inch. He held his head so that he had one eye on the depth manometer and his left ear turned towards the sound room.

Two blows hit the boat broadside. More wild roaring and gurgling. Two more blows in the midst of the raging tumult.

A fresh attack, four, five detonations. Close. Marek closed his eyelids and saw projected jets of flame, towering pillars of stars, cascading sparks around the dark-red central cores, dazzling white flames, whirling Catherine wheels, bright flashes piercing the darkness.

Another gigantic fist came down and rattled the boat. The needle of the depth gauge jerked back. The lights went out and there was the sound of more breaking glass. Finally the emergency lights were extinguished.

Andras had to decide, should he take the boat down even deeper below where the last depth charges exploded or up a few metres, hoping the charges were still set for a deeper explosion. Back on the roller coaster again. The last surge made it sound as if the depth charges were forward and to port of the boat. But were they above or below?

Jersey, still holding on desperately in the control room was hit on the third dorsal vertebra, followed by another - and another, two straight punches to the back of the head and neck. This would be illegal in a boxing match, he thought.

Smoke is beginning to whirl out of the helmsman's station. To crown everything else were they going to have a fire? Were those cables beginning to smoulder. And wouldn't that cause short circuits?

Everything was wet, covered in condensation. "Driving

shaft gaskets making water!" someone shouted from the stern. Followed immediately by "valve leaking." No one was paying much attention. Why bother about which bloody valve it might be.

Four more detonations in quick succession, then the mad gurgle and roar of the water rushing back into huge hollows torn out by the depth charges.

The next detonation slammed the boat again and sobbing could be heard from the control room. Was it one of the young midshipmen? Surely someone was going to have a fit of hysterics?

"Don't worry chaps," said a cheerful Tadeusz, staggering among the crew. "If you can hear the explosions and feel the vibrations you are still alive." All he got back was a few doubtful looks.

Marek tensed his stomach muscles as if to protect his organs against a ton of pressure. It was some minutes before he dared release his left hand from its grip on the pipe. It rose of its own volition and brushed across his forehead. Cold sweat. His whole back felt equally clammy. Was it fear? There was a sour taste in his mouth and a dull pressure somewhere in his head. He held his breath, but it only made the pressure worse.

Eryk , still holding on grimly, thought he saw the deck plates rise, but it is seconds before he heard their metallic clatter mixed with a yowling, groaning sound and a high pitched screech. The pressure hull! It cannot be anything else. The boat heaved and pitched in the rearing eddies. Men staggered against one another. Another double blast. The boat groaned. Clattering scraping sounds.

And, suddenly, silence. A comprehensive silence.

Seconds stretched to minutes, the minutes pass. Slowly life began to return to something like normality as each man tried to sort himself out, checking his body parts to make sure they were still operating. They looked across at each other with sickly smiles. The unspoken question: How the hell are we still alive?

"Everyone all right" Andras asked in a calm. authoritative voice. There is a murmur of doubtful assent.

* * *

It was another two hours, spent trying to bring some order to the interior of the submarine, before Andras decided to return to periscope depth to check on the situation.

He swept round the horizon in silence, and then: "Prepare to surface."

It was a decision he made with some hesitation, but the batteries desperately needed re-charging and that would take five hours or more and there were only six hours before dawn.

"Surface," came the next order and the submarine began to pitch and roll as it rose and burst into the night, throwing water aside like a dolphin showing off. In a flurry of activity Andras threw back the hatch and, amid a torrent of water, clambered on to the bridge followed by two lookouts. A quick look around. Nothing. The sea had an empty feel about it.

Andras, using instincts honed over several years at sea, told him that all was well. He had no inner sense of danger.

Piotr, the duty Officer of the Watch, came on the bridge expecting Andras to immediately go below after a quick discussion on the situation. But Andras stayed on the bridge, clearly wishing to talk.

"It's been a bit tricky, "he said.

"I've known better," Piotr replied.

"What about the destroyers, do you think we got them?

"Difficult to say," said Andras, "We certainly got two hits on something. Whether they were both on the same destroyer or one on each, or on something else, I don't know.

I think if we'd sunk something they would still be looking for us. At least they would still have patrols boats searching."

"Unless they thought they had sunk us."

"Well, whatever, we've got to decide what we do next," Andras suggested,"get Andrzej and Jersey to carry out an inventory of damage and what we've got left, fuel, water, the lot. As soon as possible,." Piotr nodded.

"Officers to meet me in the control room in 30 minutes, with Ryzard and Robert. Their experience will be useful. We'll make a decision then."

Although the damage seemed superficial with nothing seriously threatening the life of the submarine, the report on resources was short and worrying.

It was a sombre meeting. The end of the attack and the period of quiet had allowed both the officers and the crew to reflect on the news about Poland that had broken just before the attack.

Andras looked into the face of those present. He could see they were totally exhausted, both physically and mentally.

"We've been talking about future plans. I don't think we have very much choice. We could put into a Swedish port and finish our war, but I know that none of you would accept that as a solution. Obviously we cannot go on cruising the Baltic hoping to find a target for the four torpedoes we've got left, as we're running short of everything and conditions in the submarine are becoming impossible. I believe that the only choice we have is to get out of the Baltic and try to get to England, join the Royal Navy and start fighting the enemy seriously."

There was a moment of silence.

"You won't get an argument from any of us," said Tomasz with conviction. "There isn't a choice. We all want to go on fighting in view of what has happened and that is the only way." The others nodded sombrely.

"If I may contribute," said Ryzard, conscious of the fact that he was only a non-commissioned Chief Petty Officer. Andras nodded.

"Getting out of the Baltic is easily said, but if not impossible, it is extremely difficult. The only way, considering our condition and lack of resources, is through 'The Sound'. It is 70 kilometers long and is very narrow, less than four kilometers wide, and can be as little as seven metres deep. Although, theoretically, it is either neutral or territorial water, it is full of ships, including German warships which will be looking for us. The only way to try to do it is to stick as closely as possible to the coastline where, as I say, the water is shallow and we will not be able to submerge. There will be no way to confirm whether ships are friends or foes," Ryzard explained. "But," he added, not wanting the officers to think he lacked enthusiasm, "I agree we should try it."

"Thank you for that encouraging summary," Andras replied, smiling broadly. "Would you be happier if we put you ashore first?"

"No, Sir, I cannot speak either Danish or Swedish," Ryzard laughed. "And I'm not that strong a swimmer."

"It should be pointed out," said Robert optimistically, "that going through 'The Sound' without being spotted, was achieved by a Royal Navy submarine during the First World War."

"Then we can certainly do it," declared Mucha emphatically.

* * *

EIGHT

Piotr was sitting quietly alone in the small officers' mess thinking. For the first time for days there was no immediate pressure. The *'Eagle'* was cruising on the surface at medium speed. Visibility was obscured by a heavy mist, bad enough to persuade Andras to post four lookouts on the bridge, one for each quarter. Andrzej, a noted alert man of action, was Officer of the Watch.

Andras appeared at the door. "May I come in and sit down?" he asked, conscious of the fact that the officers' mess was a private place for them. As much as any place could be private in this crowded vessel.

"Of course," replied Piotr, half standing up. The two men, the Captain and his right hand man had great appreciation for each other. In any other profession they would have been close friends of equal standing, but in a submarine there was always the question of rank. Both men understood this and would do nothing to indicate anything different, even when they were alone together.

"The news was bloody awful," Andras said eventually.

Piotr nodded, "It could not be worse." They sat silent for a moment, each with their own thoughts.

"You come from Warsaw don't you?" Piotr asked. Andras nodded. "So do Tomasz, Slawomir and Marcin."

"Your wife there?" Andras nodded again,

"As far as I know. She may have moved to Lodz to be with her parents. They might have insisted that she go and stay with them."

"It's a hell of a worry for you," Piotr commented.

"It's worse than that," Andras replied. "One of the biggest problems is that she is Jewish."

Piotr was stunned. He could not think what to say.

"Andrzej's wife is Jewish too, isn't she?" was all he could think of saying.

Andras nodded: "They're cousins."

Conversation ceased as if terminated by a sudden power cut. Piotr could not think of what to say as the implication of Andras's news flashed through his mind. The import of the news from Poland and its emphasis of Nazi reaction to those of Jewish faith was too ghastly to reflect on, never mind discuss.

Andras had frightened himself by putting into words facts that he had being trying to deny.

The news report had revealed that Jews were being rounded up and sent to camps, but it has not made clear whether that was only men or women, or both. Piotr tried to think of how he would feel in a similar situation, but he found it impossible.

Andras could see that Piotr was finding it difficult. "You're from Kazalin if I remember right," he said,

"Yes," replied Piotr, glad of the change of subject.

"Married too?"

"Was."

"Oh!"

"She left me about three months ago. She was fed up with my devotion to the Navy. Said she wanted a different life."

"I know the problem," Andras interrupted.

"I didn't think there was anyone else. She couldn't understand why I always put the Navy first. But with war on the horizon I had no choice. She couldn't see that it was not just a question of me being loyal to my job, but that I was protecting my country and her."

"None of us could possibly change," said Piotr. "Jersey was the same. He was told that his father was dying so he should stay at home. But how could he have possibly done that."

"Well, it's water under the bridge now," said Andras with a sigh. "God knows what we will find if we ever get out of this. I think some of the crew have already given up. They haven't given up fighting, but they've given up thinking about any future or whether they will ever see Poland and home again."

"And if we do go back what will we find? More to the point, who will still be around?"

Andras stood up. "Let's not get despondent. We've got to keep the crew's spirits up. And our own," he smiled.

Piotr stood up as Andras moved out. "Thanks for the chat," said the Captain.

Similar conversations were going on in all parts of the ship. Card games were lethargic, with none of the usual vociferous arguments and comments. Most of them were playing the popular game Black Queen, where the cards were divided between the players, they then had to pass three cards to the player on their left. The Queen of Spades and other court cards in that suit had penalty points which counted against them. When the game has ended and tricks collected, the points are added up and, of course, the one with the most points lost and pays up. It is when the three cards are passed and are found to be those with unpleasant implications that the comments usually started. You could either pass the penalty cards to the person on your left, and risk them being given back to you during the play, or you could hold on to them in the hope that you could play them on tricks picked up by someone else. It was a game fraught with swearing, various crudities, and vulgar comment. On this occasion it was played almost in silence.

* * *

'*Eagle*' continued its journey west with few alarms, the occasional sound of aircraft being the main reasons for anxiety, but the clouds provided an ideal protection. As the submarine neared the Swedish coast under clearing clouds with stars visible for the first time, the mood became uneasy.

Marek and Eryk were the lookouts on the starboard side and the first drama came from Marek, who did his best to sound controlled and efficient.

"Land ahoy, starboard side, lights visible," he called. For the first time that night there was a difference in the shades of grey of sky and sea, and between them the darker outline of land, speckled here and there with lights, some flickering.

"Look at this," he said to Eryk pointing to the illuminated land, "this is peace."

The remark was just. Accustomed to a complete black-out, they gazed through their glasses, transfixed at the lights in houses and cottages. A moving light indicated a vehicle of some sort. On the far right was a moving necklace of lights which could be a train heading for the town or port which lay just ahead of them. A small cruise liner, brilliantly lit, was just leaving. Snatches of music from the upper deck floated through the air.

Through glasses they could see couples strolling about the decks, or nestled closely in corners. Some kind of supper dance was in progress. The sea itself became illuminated with various marker buoys and leading lights, something that they hadn't seen for a long time. It all looked like a different world, a world in which they had no place.

Andras, accompanied by Piotr, Andrzej, Mucha and Jersey, came on to the bridge to be hypnotised by the first signs of civilisation they had seen for what seemed to them like months.

"That must be Trelleborg," said Jersey, "we will soon be nearing the Sound."

"And," added Andras, "dawn will be breaking soon. Prepare to dive."

It was with deep reluctance that those on the bridge began to leave, not knowing if, or when, they might see a similar scene again. Each of them tried desperately to be the last to leave the bridge.

Andras took the boat away from the land to where he thought there might be deeper water, submerged and put her on the bottom to await the time when they would attempt the impossible.

* * *

"There must be another, easier, way out," said Mucha, slightly exasperated after the journey ahead had been described by Ryzard. As a former teacher he always felt that all questions or suggestions should be examined from every angle, before a decision is made.

"There are three ways out of the Baltic into the North Sea," Ryzard had explained. "One way, in the south, is between the Danish mainland and the island of Fuan, but it is very narrow and shallow and impossible for us. A bigger gap is between Fuan and Zealand, but it is subjected to very strong variable tides, it is dotted with dangerous reefs and, again, is quite narrow. The Sound, between Copenhagen and the Swedish coast is the only way worth trying, even though it looks impossible. As already explained it is 70 kilometres long, only four kilometres wide at its narrowest between Halsingor and Halsingborg and its maximum depth is a mere seven metres. And it will be full of ships."

"Someone said the other day that a British submarine had done it during the First World War," Mucha added questioningly.

"That's true," Ryzard conceded, "but don't forget that was in the early days of flying, there was no such thing as aerial reconnaissance and not many air attacks. Remember, depth charges had not been invented and there were no anti-submarine detection devices. I'm sorry, but it just has to be through the Sound, the Kattegat and the Skaggerak. A journey of something over 480 kilometres or so."

"Tell us about the Kattegat and Skaggerak. What do we face there?" Piotr asked.

"They won't be as difficult geographically, for the Kattegat opens up immediately we are through the Sound's narrowest gap, but it narrows to around 80 kilometres at the northern end. The worst feature of this patch of sea is the weather, there can be some very violent storms. The Skaggerak is between 120 and 140 kilometres wide, shallow on the Danish side, but deeper near the Norwegian coast. There is usually plenty of traffic in both areas, and we must expect German warships. Then we've got the North Sea. That can be rough with plenty of German ships around, but of course, the Royal Navy will be there," said Ryzard, his last remark greeted by half hearted clapping.

"Now you know," said Andras, standing. "It isn't a question of can we do it, or will we do it, it's basically a question of how long it will take us to do it. Everything is in short supply and conditions in the submarine could not be much worse. None of us has washed for several days and I need say no more about that. We haven't had a decent drink of tea for at least the same period. Most of the food is rotten, and eating the hard tack is not easy without liquid. In fact, I don't know what the hell you are all doing here," he added.

"Following our gallant Captain to the bitter end," said Tomasz with a smile.

"Glad to see you still have a sense of humour," Andras noted with a broad grin.

* * *

For the lookouts who had spent most of September being

alarmed or apprehensive whenever they saw a light on the horizon, or in the sky, the scene before them now was glittering. There were lights everywhere, lights on the land, static and moving, lights from marker buoys, lights from ships, red and green navigation lights. It was difficult to know what to report. Trying to identify the lights was beyond them.

For Andras the fear was not so much whether they would be spotted and attacked, or that they might run aground and be destroyed or captured or, when the submarine was submerged, it might be hit by a surface vessel, it was whether his ever-present fear and lack of confidence, would become obvious to the crew. He had managed to stop what he knew were the signs of indecision he showed, such as pulling at the loose skin around his finger nails, or scratching the back of his neck. It was a feeling of doubt he had experienced since he took over as Captain in Tallinn. He was supremely confident as the First Lieutenant because he knew, subconsciously, that the Captain, not him, was finally responsible. He always knew he could be a Captain one day, but now he was not only in charge of the ship, he was responsible for the lives of 54 men in an impossible situation. His decisions could determine whether they lived or died. The problem was not, he decided, a situation for which you could plan ahead. It was a matter of reacting to events, taking a pragmatic approach. And being right every time. It was, in fact, quite impossible.

Piotr had come on to the bridge and stood looking at his Captain. He knew exactly how Andras felt.

"We can do it," he told him quietly.

* * *

Acting lookouts, Chief Yeoman Zygmont and Yarwin were straining their eyes to try and establish what they were looking at, their imaginations working overtime. Suddenly Yarwin thought he saw an object, slightly darker than the rest, on the starboard beam. He blinked his eyes and looked again. It was still there. And it was moving. In the same direction. It seemed closer. He looked again. It was closer.

"Ship on the starboard beam, looks to be on a collision course," he called out in a restrained voice, sure that if he spoke too loud people on the nearby shoreline would be able to heard him.

"Stand by to dive," said Andras. Piotr and the lookouts cleared the bridge.

"Dive, dive, dive. Periscope depth," the order followed quickly.

"Up periscope, port twenty," he added after dropping into the control room and grabbing the periscope handles as they glided up. "It's a small freighter. It was on a collision course. Well done Yarwin." Yarwin's chest gained two inches in diameter.

"Slow ahead, five knots."

Andras edged the 'Eagle' along slowly at periscope depth, but when, at one stage, there was a distinct sound of scraping under the submarine he called for the engines to be stopped. They were in what they suspected, was only seven metres of water. He was grateful that the weather was overcast and there was no moon, otherwise the boat might have been visible from the air. The noise from the engines of other ships passing by was, at times, heart stopping for if a large ship had sailed directly over her she could have been hit and fatally damaged.

The strain began to tell on all of them, and there was no easing of it when Andras ordered the periscope up. The view was frightening. They were still some distance away from the narrow strait, but there were ships everywhere, including German destroyers and E-boats with searchlights piercing the horizon in every direction. Andras indicated to Piotr that he should have a look. He did so and, surprised by the activity, whistled lowly.

"We haven't discussed the possibility of a minefield in this area," he noted.

"I'm trying not to," Andras replied, "but if you look carefully over to starboard you will notice there are some areas where there are no ships. Do they know something we don't know?"

"Could be," came the dejected reply.

"Let's go up again and have a look," Andras suggested.

Slowly the submarine rose to the surface, with Piotr waiting until the control tower was clear of the water. He reached up and opened the hatch, to be greeted by the customary shower of water, and started to climb out. Abruptly he stopped, clambered down shouting

"Emergency dive" and slammed the hatch shut.

The surfacing routine was quickly reversed, the sound of water refilling the ballast tanks almost drown Piotr's voice: "We are almost alongside a bloody German destroyer," he announced breathlessly.

Andras took the submarine down only a short distance before it gently hit the bottom and stopped engines.

"I have no idea whether they spotted us," Piotr added. "I didn't have time to look, but it seemed to me, on first reaction, that it was stationery."

"Well, there's no sound of an engine," Andras confirmed "And we'll soon know if they saw us. A depth charge or two at this moment would not be good."

There was total silence as everyone waited for the first, and probably the last, explosion. Minutes passed and slow breathing was continued on a steady pattern.

"We'll wait awhile before we try again," Andras announced. No-one argued.

An hour later, again at periscope depth, Andras took a very slow, careful, look around, particularly on the port side where the destroyer was reported to have been.

"All clear," he said with some certainty, "take her up"

Once again the *'Eagle'* rose with, this time, Tomasz taking the lead role. He moved even more quickly than his colleague, but this time there was no problem. On the port side, no ship or lights except those visible on the land.

"The sea is absolutely clear on the port side," he reported. "It's odds on it's a minefield.

"I'm going to go ahead very slowly," Andras told him, "until we get as close to the narrows as we can, while we surface and charge the batteries, and then spend the day on the bottom before attacking the narrows at night."

It was a statement that did not require a comment.

* * *

Eryk and Marek were assigned as lookouts on the grounds that they were both young and therefore, theoretically, had the best eyesight. It would also be good experience for them as potential officers. Huddled up in heavy coats and woollen helmets they stood as close as they could to each while still able to keep an efficient watch.

"I wonder what out parents would say if they could see us now," said Eryk conversationally. He knew immediately that he had said the wrong thing, for he sensed Marek stiffening and fixing him with his steady gaze. He understood, he had the same feeling himself.

They both recalled the perilous position their parents were now in. They could be worse off than the pair of them. They were from Tczew and Sopot, both near Gdansk and therefore in the midst of the German attack on the route of the battering ram as it smashed its way across Poland. Eryk's father was headmaster at the local high school, Marek's owned a company which manufactured and sold marine equipment. Neither would be of much interest to the Germans. But that was assuming that the latter had simply one intent - to go straight through to Warsaw. Both Eryk and Marek knew that their mothers would be terrified.

"Sorry," said a contrite Eryk "it was the wrong thing to say."

"No matter," Marek replied. "I think they will be more concerned with their own problems. They've probably already given us up for lost." God, he thought to himself, what an awful thing to believe, that my mother and father no longer think I exist. He shivered, and it was not through the cold.

Both returned their attention to the scene facing them. It was a murky picture, overhead dark rain-filled clouds sped across the sky, beneath them a grey sea became agitated by a rising wind. On one side dozens of ships, some with navigation lights, others simply dark shapes. On the other the blank threat of an empty sea and the portent of a hidden danger.

'Eagle' completed its tentative journey through the night with fewer alarms than expected, thanks largely to the weather which, in different circumstances, would be described as appalling, but on this occasion was most welcome.

When it submerged, as dawn broke over the dismal scene, there was a moment of concern when the submarine hit something as it touched bottom, only six metres down. Once again they feared an explosion would follow, but nothing happened, and it was concluded that they had probably ended up alongside an old wreck.

As night fell, Andras called the crew together around the central area. "We are about to attempt to go through the narrow strait between Copenhagen and Malmo, a busy stretch of water which will include a number of German warships. We are unable to go through submerged because the water is generally too shallow, The one thing in our favour is the atrocious weather, with total cloud cover and heavy rain. This will not only reduce visibility to a minimum but will discourage lookouts from being fully alert.

"It is going to be extremely dangerous and the chances of getting through are, at best, fifty:fifty - no, Jake, no betting - and I am anxious to give the greatest number possible the chance to come through this alive. I only want volunteers to stay below performing vital duties, in the engine room and control room. Basically, the rest will be on deck or on the bridge," he stopped talking to allow the import of what he had said to sink in. "Any questions?"

"How long do you think it will take us to reach safety?" asked Tadeus. "I don't want to spend too long getting wet, I might catch a cold," he added, hoping his joke would break some of the tension.

"Having stood close to you recently I would suggest that the wetter you get the better, and that goes for everyone" said Andras indirectly indicating the state of the crew who had almost forgotten what washing was. "Between three and four hours, if all goes well. We cannot increase speed because I don't want us to leave a wash which can be seen."

"What happens if we are hit?" asked Hreinski, trying his luck. Andras looked at him and smiled.

"I guessed that the intellectual question would come from you," said Andras amid laughter. "The idea of being on deck is so that if we are hit you will be able to swim to safety, either to Denmark, Sweden or to a neutral ship. You don't need to be told the disadvantage of swimming to a German ship, do you?" The last question was greeted by more laughter, and an embarrassed smile from Hreinski.

"Dress as warmly as you can and make your way upsides as soon as possible," Andras ordered. "Good luck."

Jersey, Robert, Lukasz and Guayne manned the engine room; Coxswain Stefan, Bosun Jacek, Tadeus and Andrzej with Marek took vital roles below, led by Piotr.

The weather on the surface was every bit as bad as forecast, and within seconds all those out of the submarine were soaking wet, cold and uncomfortable. Still, they told themselves, after grumbling enthusiastically, it might save their lives.

Andras and his two official lookouts peered into the gloom ahead. They passed several ships, but the deck of the submarine was so low it could not be seen from a normal surface ship. The proximity of one ship, a German destroyer, made them anxious and caused a slight alteration of course away from it.

Suddenly a searchlight piercing the gloom swung across the horizon towards them.

"Here we go," said Andras, just as the beam was cut off. Seconds later a second searchlight flashed on just astern of them and swept away.

"God is in His heaven," muttered Andras.

Unbelievably they were suddenly level with Copenhagen on the port side and Malmo on the starboard. Both were brightly lit, the first such display most of the crew had seen for weeks, and they stared in wonder, all fear temporarily forgotten.

"I hope our silhouette does not show up against this bright background," Andras said quietly.

The shadow of another ship, a small freighter, was coming towards them. Concern about it disappeared when it abruptly turned on its navigation lights.

Andras grunted: "Must be a neutral. But why did they switch on their lights just then?" he asked no-one in particular. "Must have thought they saw something ahead of them," he answered his own question.

The *'Eagle'* made steady progress, a black steel tube gliding under raven-black clouds through a dark choppy sea. The crew crouched low on the deck in torrential rain, frozen bodies wrapped in sodden clothes, concentrating on the murky night enveloping them.

They were surrounded by dark shapes which could bring to a sudden end their latest trials.

Minds became concentrated when another black steel tube

was seen looming not a 100 metres away. Another submarine! It could only be a U-boat! Around 40 pairs of eyes were fixed on the sight as nerves tensed and reaction was expected. But the two vessels slipped past each other and there was no incident.

"We must have been hidden by the black of the land behind us," said a relieved Tomasz.

The bright lights of visible civilisation slowly fell astern. The gap between the two coastlines began to broaden. At last they were in the Kattegat.

"We"ve done it, at least the first and worst part," called Andras quietly,"Everyone below, as quick as you like." A muttered cheer greeted his order as the crew began to quietly scramble down to the comparative comfort of their messes.

* * *

The general feeling of well-being, following the safe passage through the Sound, was gently suppressed by the officers on Andras's instructions. It was pointed out that they may have completed what was the most dangerous part of the journey, but they still had the Kattegat and Skaggerak to negotiate. That the water was still shallow was proved beyond argument when the 'Eagle' was caught by the searchlight of a torpedo boat, and dived. At six metres it shuddered as the dive came to an abrupt termination, and while the crew was struggling to regain their feet it bounced to the surface and then dropped four metres, once again finding the seabed. It came to rest more or less upright.

"Are we trying to attract attention to ourselves?" muttered a bruised Dasay.

"We should have succeeded by now," Marek responded.

Indeed at four metres the periscope standards were still above the water, but fortunately the two grey steel tubes must have been invisible against the background of a grey sea and were not spotted by the fast moving torpedo boat.

But their close association with the sea bed had not ended. It was repeated shortly afterwards, but this time with more serious consequences. This time it was hard enough to shear all the blades off the starboard propeller making it useless.

"That's buggered it," Robert grunted.

"It's not done any good," Jersey agreed. "We don't carry any oars do we?"

"I'll check," Robert laughed. "But we should be able to manage with one prop for a short time."

The feeling began to percolate through the crew that they had used up all their luck during the weeks in the Baltic. Andras did his best to suppress this view, but he was not helped when, as dawn was breaking, and they were still on the surface, a lookout reported three aircraft coming up fast.

Confirmation that the *Eagle's* luck had not yet changed for the better came when Andras in the control room, ordered an emergency dive. Officer of the Watch Tomasz, was the last to leave the bridge. As he stepped through the hatch into the conning tower his foot slipped and he let go of the hatch with one hand and grabbed the rim with the other to save himself. The hatch came crashing down and, with a sharp cry of agony, trapped his hand. The submarine was still submerging and water was pouring into the conning tower, the hatch could not be closed properly and water was gushing in with increasing pressure making it impossible for Tomasz to free his hand. There was a danger that the submarine would take on too much water and eventually sink.

While most of those around stood looking on in horror Marcin, in the control room heard the cry, took in the scene immediately, raced to the conning tower ladder and climbed up alongside Tomasz. When he got half way up, he lifted his legs above his head until he was upside down and, holding on to one of the rungs with his hands, and thrust his legs up against the hatch.

"Increase speed, quickly," he shouted as loud as he could against the sound of rushing water. Jersey, at the motor control immediately understood the situation and thrust the engines ahead. They reacted quickly, and suddenly the submarine surged forward momentarily reducing the pressure of the water on the hatch. Marcin, using all his strength thrust his legs upwards against the hatch, moving it fractionally, enough to allow Tomasz to pull his hand free, close the hatch with other and seal it. Tomasz stumbled down while Marcin returned to the upright position and dropped down to the deck. The two men, drenched and breathless, looked at each other.

"Thank you," Tomasz said gratefully to Marcin. "You saved my life," he added quietly.

"He saved the submarine," Andras added, increasing Marcin's embarrassment.

He was subjected to an outbreak of back patting and a flood of congratulations while Kacek took Tomasz to the so-called sick bay.

"That was a remarkable reaction," Andras told Marcin, "bloody remarkable."

"Well, I knew simply trying to push it up would not work and I know my strongest feature are my legs. It seemed the only way was to try and relieve pressure by jerking the submarine forward so that the direction of the water was slightly changed to flowing astern. Luckily it worked," Marcin replied modestly.

"It certainly did," Andras agreed.

Tomasz's agony was Kacek's opportunity to show what he had learned. He straightened the fingers, four of which seemed to be broken, and bound each of them with a splint. Then he bound all four together. He apologised for not having any painkillers.

"That's okay," said Tomasz cheerfully. "Will I be able to play the piano?"

"I would think so, after they have mended and the stiffness

has gone they should be back to normal," said Kacek, having no idea what the outcome of his efforts would be.

"That's good," said Tomasz, "because I couldn't play it before."

* * *

As Tomasz walked back to the small wardroom where there was more room to relax, he met Marcin. They looked at each other without speaking.

"Thank you again," Tomasz said.

"It was a pleasure," Marcin replied. "I'm glad I was able to do something."

"I think that more than balances everything out," Tomasz suggested. "Shall we forget the past?"

"It seems pretty pointless to worry about what has happened. We've got enough to worry about what is going to happen in the future. I am sorry for what did. I did not know the real circumstances, although I know that is no excuse."

"As you say, what has gone has gone," Tomasz agreed. "Are you still in touch with Alina?"

Marcin smiled self-effacingly. "She left me," he said. "She found someone more acceptable, someone who was not devoted to the Polish Navy."

Tomasz smiled. "We can be friends then?" Marcin nodded. Tomasz looked at his damaged hands.

"You will forgive me if we don't shake on it," Marcin grabbed his left hand with both of his and held them strongly.

* * *

The following day the *'Eagle'* left the Kattegat and moved into the Skaggerak near the Norwegian coast where the water was deeper and safer.

Andras sent for Slawomir. Send a message to the British Admiralty in plain language, we'll have to risk it being picked up.

"This is the Polish submarine 'Eagle', Captain Andras. We have broken out of the Baltic and are roughly fifty kilometers south-east of Kristiansand heading for Rosyth. We are badly damaged, almost out of fuel, desperately short of supplies, no navigation equipment and no charts. Escort would be welcome."

Less than an hour later Slawomior came out of the wireless office holding a piece of paper. It was from the Admiralty.

"Congratulations. Well done. Destroyer escorts on their way."

* * *

NINE

The following day dawned overcast and calm, calm enough to persuade Andras to take a risk and stay on the surface with Piotr, and two lookouts maintaining a constant search for any sign of an enemy. He was concerned because his signal to the British Admiralty was in plain language and would almost certainly have been picked up by the Germans.

When, in mid-morning, the sound of aircraft disturbed the peace and calm of the day, quick moves were made to vacate the bridge and submerge, but an instinct persuaded Andras to stay on the surface in case the aircraft sounds could be the RAF or Fleet Air Arm looking for them. Andras watched the approaching aircraft with growing misgivings. Was it British or German?

His fears disappeared thanks to a lookout's cry: "Ship on the horizon dead ahead. Signalling."

Was this it? Was this the moment when, after six weeks at sea, they were no longer alone?

"Signal Sir," said Zygmont reading the flashing light from the oncoming destroyer.

"Polish submarine 'Eagle' I presume. Shall I take your hand and lead you home?"

"Reply" said Andras, "Your help would be gratefully received Stop Our steps are very uncertain. Stop. Thank you for rushing to our *aid Stop you are a welcome sight. Stop. You lead Stop I will follow."*

Zygmont started again as the destroyer's light continued to flash: "*Congratulations on your escape Stop Anything you urgently need?*"

Andras laughed, tell him: "*Everything Stop Desperately need a change of diet as we have no food left. Stop We have not had any tea for two weeks Stop You can forget the cream cakes.*"

"Will send an emergency package Stop Coming alongside," was the answer.

As the aircraft patrolled above them the destroyer *'Valorous'* raced towards the *'Eagle'*, swept past and then with a majestic sweeping turn came up alongside. A rope, fired across to the *'Eagle's'* bridge, was grabbed by Guayne and Hreinski who had been sent to the bridge to receive anything sent over by the destroyer.

On the end of the rope was the start of the transferring gear – two ropes, one with a pulley which allowed the second, carrying several substantial packages, to be pulled over.

Guayne and Hreinski needed no encouragement to enthusiastically haul the packages across and drop them onto the bridge. The first was quickly opened by Piotr who found a large box of tea, tinned milk, boxes of bacon and eggs and two bottles of rum.

"Incredible," said Piotr. He ordered them to be taken below and handed to Jacek, the Bosun. "He will know what to do."

"Tell him to feed those off watch immediately, and then change watches as quickly as possible," Andras ordered. "That will do morale some good," was his notable understatement to Piotr.

Marek looked at the rum with fond memories. It transported him back to the civilised world. When he was with the Royal Navy on his training exercise he was able to take part in the Navy tradition of noontime 'Up Spirits' when each member of the crew was given a tot of rum in the true traditions of Nelson's Navy. Usually watered down on a ratio of 2:1 or, sometimes 3:1, it was not only a much cherished tradition in the Royal Navy, but, if the rules were broken and it was saved and not drunk immediately, the tot, or part of it. could be used as a powerful tool of bribery at a later date. It had two currencies, 'sippers', which was a closely observed short sip enough to give the taste, or 'gulpers' an even more strictly observed single swallow. Many an extra run ashore was bought from the person whose leave it was to allow someone else to go on 24-hour leave. Some could be persuaded to do any washing that needed doing, or even take responsibility for someone's watch. Marek's description to the *'Eagle's'* crew, with the promise that it would be adopted when they joined the British fleet, did much to bolster the already high morale.

The atmosphere in the submarine was unlike anything in the past six weeks. Ryzard put it into words. Gazing into space and speaking aloud to himself, but, of course, heard by all those around him.

"It's like awakening from a bloody nightmare. The dark oblivion of sleep when terrible things happen, you lie full of fear and dreaded anticipation, with no control over events, waiting for the next awful thing to occur and then, suddenly, you are awake, the black curtain disappears. It is daylight, the sun is shining and you look out of the window at a world that is normal, in which you are in control of your thoughts and actions."

Murmurs of agreement and understanding came from those within earshot. Ryzard started, surprised that he had been expressing himself aloud and that people had heard what he had been thinking.

"Well put," said Andras who had been among those listening," but although we now feel in control again, with the terrors behind us, we must not forget that we are still in a war situation and cannot afford to relax. True, we are no longer alone, we have a highly professional escort, but we still have to be prepared to defend ourselves.

The sobering reminder that they were still at war, and in danger, was accepted stoically and renewed the crew's determination to complete what they set out to do, fight and defeat the enemy.

***

Further conversations with the destroyer ensued during which Andras pointed out that although they had around 300 miles to go to Rosyth they were incapable of steaming at more than 10 knots on the surface, and five knots below, because of their desperate fuel situation and their broken propeller. There was no way they could refuel at sea for it was almost certain that U-boats would be around, and the opportunity to sink a submarine and a near stationary oil tanker would be too much for them. It was agreed that *'Eagle'* would stay on the surface with the destroyer circling around it so that its hydrophones, and those of the submarine, could pick up any sounds made by enemy U-boats.

Deservedly the near two-day journey towards Britain was uneventful. It seemed to the *'Eagle's'* crew that the escorting destroyer was weaving a safety curtain around them as it continued circling. The feeling grew stronger that at last their luck really had changed.

As dusk was falling on the second day a cry from one of the lookouts alerted the whole crew. 'Land ahoy!' came the cry.

It gave Guayne, the lookout, particular excitement. Since reading seafaring stories in his boyhood he had always wanted to cry 'land ahoy!'.

"England at last," shouted Yarwin on the bridge.

"Scotland, actually," corrected Ryzard.

"Well, it's Britain, whatever," snapped Yarwin, annoyed that his elation had been tempered.

"There are no lights visible," observed Dasay among the crowd assembling on the deck. He was remembering the brilliantly lit picture of the coasts of Denmark and Sweden as they passed.

"You may not know it," said Ryzard with a hint of sarcasm in his voice, "but there is a war on and Britain is one of the combatants."

"Sorry, I forgot," said an apologetic Dasay, "but I was remembering what it was like when we went through the Sound." Other members of the crew were reminded of that nerve-racking experience.

Only the Engineer Jersey quietly recalled that it was seven weeks since they had fled the battered port of Gydnia and the Germans. It was unbelievable what had happened during that period.

Slowly the *'Eagle'* headed into the Firth of Forth as the *'Valorous'* signalled. *"I am now leaving you Stop Continue up the Firth until you get to the Forth Bridge Stop Turn starboardt and you will see the Rosyth submarine base Stop I am sure a warm welcome awaits you Stop Good luck."*

"Thank you for all your help Stop It was invaluable Stop Good luck to you Stop." Andras signalled back. With that the destroyer whooped its siren and raced off, free at last from the restrictive speed of the submarine.

* * *

The voyage up the Firth of Forth became more of a cruise for the crew of the *'Eagle'*. They watched transfixed as they passed the gannet-infested Bass Rock, a notable navigation feature of the Firth, on the port side. An escort squadron of flying seagulls took off to keep watch over them or, more realistically, to search for any food thrown overboard. They picked up the pilot, and admired the picturesque Fife coast with its background of the Cliesh and Lomond Hills to starboard. The greens, browns and gold of the Scottish countryside were like a landscape painting on view to be admired.

Before long they could see the Scottish capital Edinburgh, and its port of Granton, and the imposing structure of the Forth railway bridge, under which the submarine sailed with its neck-stretching crew taking in the intricate structure of its ironwork.

"They are constantly painting that," explained Ryzard, "they start at one end and when they reached the other they go back to the beginning and start again."

"Sounds like a bloody waste of time," commented Dasay.

"It has to be done that way," snapped Ryzard ,"to protect the ironwork."

Then the submarine base and its depot ship became the ultimate welcome sight. To the surprise of all aboard the *'Eagle'* the decks of every vessel in the harbour, jetties and the piers were crowded with cheering sailors. Everything else was forgotten.

"What a bloody marvellous welcome," Piotr said to Andras, who was too emotionally moved to answer. After a moment of stunned surprise those aboard the submarine began to wave back and start cheering.

The pilot brought the submarine alongside the depot ship where the Base Captain was waiting to greet them.

"You can see how we feel about you and your safe arrival," he said nodding towards the cheering crowds. "You are very welcome and many congratulations on your achievement," he added enthusiastically shaking Andras's hand. "I have been asked by the Flag Officer Submarines, who is sorry he cannot be here, to pass on a message." *Your achievement is amongst the highest of any submarine service. Instead of sailing directly to a*

Swedish port, or straight to Britain you returned to your operations sector in the Baltic. You did so in spite of the fact that you could have asked for internment in a neutral port. In fact, when they tried to carry out that manoeuvre you and your crew bravely risked escape. You did not have any success in sinking German ships during your time in the Baltic, but it is well known that you did succeed in spreading alarm in the German ranks, and tied up many units searching for you for many weeks."

"Thank you for that very generous welcome, and for the much appreciated message. We did what we thought we had to do and we are now ready to take up the fight against the enemy," said Andras, whose grasp of the Engliah language had often been commented upon..

"I think you may have a day or two off before you return to action. I understand you have some damage which will need attention, and I am sure your crew needs a damn good rest. The commander of the depot ship will take over the *'Eagle'* and arrange to effect the necessary repairs. You, your officers, and crew will be accommodated on the depot ship. You will all be given medicals and any treatment necessary, but the urgent need is for you and your men to have some rest in comfortable surroundings, and we can offer that." the Base Captain told him.

The crew remained in a daze, surrounded as they were by hundreds of new friends in a new and strange world.

"You've been here before?" Dasay asked Marek.

"No, I was on the battleship *'Nelson'* in the Mediterranean, but I do know about British depot ships, they're bloody marvellous. There'll be separate cabins for the officers and messes and accommodation for the whole crew. It will like living in an hotel on leave, although I expect they'll find work for us to do. They're fully equipped with workshops to handle everything. I think they'll be able to repair all our damage."

Marek noticed that Lukasz was listening intently. "You'll be okay for they'll have a chapel and a chaplain so you'll be able to get all religious." He noticed too, that Kacek was also listening and added, looking at him with a steady gaze: "We'll get proper medical attention and be able to put right everything you've buggered up."

Kacek stared at him with disdain, not appreciating his sense of humour even though he knew it was a joke.

* * *

It was in total silence that the crew gathered their few possessions and moved off the submarine to their new temporary quarters on the depot ship. Although everyone knew they would return in the near future, they felt as though they were abandoning a seriously injured member of the crew. 'Eagle' was not just a ship, it was their home. They had been through hell together. It was an integral member of the family, one who could have its moments of anger when being battered by depth charges, impatient when it was not being handled properly, but serene when ploughing through a calm sea on a sun drenched day. It had been badly damaged in the past few weeks, the bow had been badly dented in Tallinn harbour, its bottom badly scraped, and probably dented, in shallow water where they had sought safety, and its starboard propeller had been smashed in the Sound. But all the time it did its best, uncomplaining, never refusing to obey an order. Its interior was an abomination, filthy, smelly, damp and strewn with the debris caused by human life. But again, no complaints. It had brought them through to safety. The crew not only appreciated what the 'Eagle' had done for them, but they would always be eternally grateful to the men who had built her.

The contrast when they boarded the depot ship was one of awesome astonishment. The mess deck assigned to them, six wooden tables, each seating eight men with room to move around them and, above all a high degree of cleanliness. Everything had been scrubbed clean. They were to learn later that they would be the ones that would have to do the scrubbing in future. There was a faint aroma of disinfectant, they thought, or was it just cleanliness.

Other shattering innovations, to them, included a shower room with room for up to six men to use them at the same time, lavatories, and a washroom in which to do their laundry, and an area to stow hammocks when not in use. No-one knew what to say, they did not have the words to describe the transformation in their lifestyle.

Eryk looked around the mess, and then at Marek, who was on the other side of the table. "You are further away from me than you have been for over a month," he said in wonder.

"Speak up I can't hear you," shouted Marek.

"I feel very strange," said Yarwin, "Very odd."

"You are very strange, and very odd," contributed Dasay

"I feel strange too," Marek agreed. "It's the relief from tension, the fact that there is nothing to worry about, nothing nerve wracking to occupy your mind. We have all been tense all day and every day for well over a month. Now it's all gone, we're relaxed, but we'll get used to it. Before long we'll be worried that we've got nothing to worry about. Anyway we'll soon be back in action.

Marek, Eryk and Yarwin received a further shock when they found themselves assigned to a cabin with three bunks. As Officer Cadets they knew they were entitled to some perks, but this was unexpected.

The officers were also astounded for they each had their own cabin, at last they could be alone, really alone. Although the cabins were small, they were large enough to them to spread out, had space in which to think, and not have to have relationships with someone else every hour of the day.

All of them, without exception, found there was a

drawback to this new found solitude. It gave them time to think. To think not only about the struggles they had to overcome in the North Sea, but more worryingly, to think about their families back in Poland.

It was a totally changed situation. Since the war had broken out, and they had been trapped in the Baltic, they felt themselves to still be an integral part of Poland. They were in a steel box full of dangers and difficulties in the same way as their families on the mainland. Now, for the time being, they were safe and comfortable. Their families were not.

Much to their surprise someone had brought a collection of old Polish newspapers for them to look through. Old they may be, but they were passed from hand to hand and eagerly scanned.

After hearing the latest news from Poland, there was much discussion on the cruelty of the Germans and, more particularly, of the Russians who were generally hated. Some joined in the discussion with enthusiasm, others went silent as they began, once again, to think about the horrors their families had been, and were, going through.

Now, they were virtually free. They were back in the free world, a world which had not yet discovered the realities of war. The feeling of freedom was hard to come to terms with. Any realisation of the happy, carefree situation they were now in was overlaid with sub-conscious feelings that it was wrong while their families still suffered.

* * *

Andras, finding himself largely on his own, found himself reliving his last visit to his home in Warsaw. when he was shocked to find that not only were his wife and mother not speaking to each other, they had decided to split the house in two and live alone in the own halves.

"What the hell is going on?" he asked his mother, horrified.

"It's for the best," his Mother replied comfortingly, "Alekzandra is impossible to live with, so in order to stop the arguments and continual disagreements we decided to separate."

"That's ridiculous," Tadeusz had snapped angrily, just as Alekzandra came into the room.

"I know that Alex is not impossible to live with and I know from long experience that you are not impossible. You are both grown women who should know better, you are not over emotional teenage girls. I am going back to sea soon and there is almost certain to be a war. I do not want to have to worry about another war going on at home. I love you both dearly and the best way you can help me is by loving and looking after each other."

His speech seemed to break the ice. They seemed to understand what he was saying and eventually embraced each other. The remainder of his stay passed relatively peacefully and, hopefully, it seemed that the problem was solved. After hearing the latest news from Poland, he realised that the outlook was as bad as it could be. He told himself he must find out more about the situation in Warsaw, but, he cautioned, on the other hand, ignorance could be bliss.

Piotr too was reflecting on his marital arrangements, and the fact that he no longer had a wife. When he did received her letter saying she had found someone else, and asking for a divorce, his immediate reaction had been to be defiant. Not a chance, he thought. But with Poland crumbling, and families being split asunder by death and disaster, his problems seemed infinitesimal. How important was his marriage in the scheme of things? What was the point of fighting back when clearly you were no longer wanted. His first priority was to get *'Eagle'* ready for sea and back in action, he angrily told himself.

* * *

Kacek was a bundle of nerves when he was ordered to report to the Base Commander's office. As far as he could remember he hadn't done anything wrong, but he may be getting into trouble for his diagnosis of the Captain's condition, and he might have buggered up Tomasz's hand. He was surprised to find that Andras was already there, accompanied by a Royal Navy commander who had red stripes between his gold rings indicating he was probably a surgeon.

"Good to see you Kacek," the Base Commander welcomed him. "I hear you have done some good work. This is Commander Taylor our Medical Officer," he indicated the RN officer who smiled and put out a welcoming hand.

"I congratulate you for what you did for Tomasz. It seems his hand is mending very well, and although it is too early so say, it seems unlikely that there will be any long lasting after effects. And you've had no medical training?" It was a question rather than a statement.

"No, Sir, although my father is a doctor I have no knowledge or ambitions in that area I was just doing a job to help the crew."

"Really," the Commander sounded surprised. "You certainly did that. You seem to have some knowledge and some ability. I had it in mind to offer you the chance of training at our medical school, we need good men. It might lead to promotion."

Kacek paused before replying, the implications flashing through his mind.

"Thank you, Sir, it is very kind of you, but I would rather stay on the *'Eagle'*. In the past weeks we have become a very close family. We will be going back into action shortly and I would rather be with them. If I'm wanted," he added hastily.

Andras looked at him and smiled: "I know what you mean Kacek, but personal feelings are not considered in the Navy. As far as I am concerned you are an important member of the crew. But as you know the final decision does not lie with me. Others decide who will comprise the next crew." he added gently.

"I would like to take my chance," Kacek persisted.

The Commander joined in:"Anyway, well done. Tomasz has a lot to thank you for," he said, ending the meeting.

* * *

The crew had difficulty in recognising each other when they came together for the next meeting. Clean shaven, hair cut and new clothes, and already looking healthier, they were a different bunch from the dirty, scruffy, undisciplined mob when they had last been together. Most of the conversations comprised insults as they commented on each other's appearance.

Most of the actual meeting was spent listening to a base officer explaining in slow English, so that those who did not understand could have it explained by those who did. what would be happening in the immediate future.

"Work has already started on the *'Eagle'*, repairing the mess you made of her,"   he said, smiling. "You've been bloody careless. I am not sure how long it will be before she is seaworthy again, but you will stay aboard this ship. You will follow the normal ship routine. Reveille at 0630, hammocks properly stowed by 07.00. Decks will be scrubbed between 0700 and 0730, you will be responsible for the quarter deck, and breakfast will be at 0745 until 0830 when you will repair to your training areas.

"Everyone will receive full training in their specialist areas learning how the Royal Navy does things and updating you on new developments. We have a 'Make and Mend' on Wednesday afternoon when you can do what you like.

"Shore leave will be granted between 1600 and 2300 on

weekdays and 1100 at 2300, at weekends. The liberty boat to South Queensferry leaves every 30 minutes between 1600 and 1800, and Navy transport is provided to take you into Edinburgh, dropping you at the steps of the main Post Office at the end of Princes Street, where it will pick you up every half hour from 2130 until 2300. If you miss it, it is the hell of a walk back.

"For your information there is a very good forces canteen in Princes Street near the Scott Monument which you can't miss. You will be given a month's pay at Royal Navy rates later today. If you want to save any," he was interrupted by laughter, "you can arrange an account at the Pay Office. Unfortunately we obviously cannot arrange any payments to relatives.

"Petty Officers will be giving you written details, in English and Polish, of what I have said and if you have any questions, ask them. Enjoy yourselves, you've earned it."

* * *

The first shore leave trip into Edinburgh left the crew of the 'Eagle' awestruck, especially those from the small towns and villages of Poland. As the coach raced past houses large and small, most with manicured and colourful gardens, the phrases "bloody hell", "God Almighty", and "Jesus Christ, look at that" were continuous as they progressed toward the city centre. The scenery down Princes Street with seemingly well-stocked shops and department stores on the left, and the view of the magnificent Edinburgh Castle and gardens on the right were absorbed in absolute silence.

"It's bloody overwhelming," said Yarwin, voicing the general view.

When they clambered off the bus at the steps of the Central Post Office they found that they were not the only people curious and fascinated; people who had been walking past stopped and gazed with interest at the group of people wearing naval uniforms not seen before.

Several British sailors had been on the bus and had been talking to their new companions and now offered to act as guides, offers which were quickly accepted. Most groups decided that the Forces Canteen would be their first target where they could get liquid refreshment - the favourite; and food - less important, and decide what they were going to do.

"Damn good job we've had a couple of days on the depot ship and got used to the food," said Janwyn, eyeing the well stocked food counter, "and are less hungry than we might have been, Slawomir would have stuffed himself stupid."

Slawomir, who was eyeing the food with hungry eyes, laughed and declared; "I will stuff myself stupid and I might, at last, put on some weight."

* * *

The fervid interest which the crew of the *'Eagle'* showed in the sights and scenes of Edinburgh was nothing compared to the curiosity shown by the local citizens in the men in a strange uniform, who spoke an incomprehensible language. Wherever they went people stopped to look at them with sympathetic interest. The uniforms may be strange, but the fact that they were walking freely in the street meant that they must be friendly.

Several people stopped to ask which Navy they were in, and when the answer came 'Polish', the attitude changed from one of passing interest to one of keen concern for, after all, when Poland was attacked by Germany, that forced Britain into the war to help them. The reaction of Edinburgh's citizens formed the basis of many humorous conversations back in the depot ship mess.

Janwyn, the 'fisherman' at Tallinn, and known as always good for a story, told of the time he and a group went into a restaurant. They were watched closely and, from time to time, noticed that other diners were looking at them, nudging and commenting quietly. Even the cooks in the kitchen gathered at the door to watch them. They found all this attention embarrassing until Janwyn decided to do some thing about it.

While someone asked for the bill he peeled an orange, sprinkled the peel with vinegar and then, as obviously as possible covered it with salt and pepper and then, very slowly, he added some of the sauce, still on the table, for luck. He then plucked a few leaves from the posy on the table and gently floated them over the mixture.

The whole dining room was watching with amazement.

At last one diner decided he had had enough, walked over and with a friendly greeting asked, "Excuse me for being rude, but we are all fascinated by what you have been preparing. How can you possibly eat what looks like a disgusting mess? Is it a Polish dish?"

"Who said I was going to eat it?" said Janwyn, smiling. He then picked up the bill, paid it, and they left, laughing. According to Janwyn, the other diners were disappointed, but eventually saw the humour of his gesture, and the reason for it.

The happy social life of Edinburgh, which was being thoroughly enjoyed by the crew, even though they knew the horrors of war were not over, was punctuated by the everyday routine of cleaning, attending classes and keeping up with the news from Poland on a regular basis. The main difficulty was separating fact from fiction, real news from ill-based rumour. Although Andras was in constant touch with Polish headquarters in London, there was little chance of getting the many questions posed by the crew answered satisfactorily.

They had known that Warsaw had fallen, but they had not been aware that the capital city had been almost destroyed. They knew that Jews were being confined in designated area of the towns, but not that they were then being sent to work camps. They had not taken on board the fact that children were being taken away from their parents, and that hundreds of civilians were being hunted like wild animals by German invaders from the west and Russians invaders from the east. Reaction to the horror inducing news varied, some tried to suppress or control their innermost thoughts as being too awful to contemplate; some tried to convince themselves that everything was being exaggerated; while others found it difficult to think about anything else, but tried to immerse themselves in the work they had to do, or in the training classes they had to attend, or by getting drunk ashore. They tried desperately hard not to get into discussions on the situation with other crew members. It was too depressing.

Andras, Tomasz, Marcin and Slawomir, those from Warsaw, rarely mentioned what was happening in their home town. All of them, particularly Andras and Andrzej, spared thoughts for their Jewish friends.

If you were a Jew in Warsaw you almost certainly lived in The Quarter - a community island surrounded by metropolitan Warsaw. It was an area of steel-proofed, many-windowed, houses huddled against each other. The cobbled streets were old and narrow. There were labyrinths of alleys, evil smelling and dark, littered with rubbish, bits of vegetables and black flecks of coal dust mixed with horse manure. It was an amalgam of pushcarts and wagons and people and noise.

More than a million people lived around Warsaw and a third of them were Jews. The Quarter was tight and warm and dark, it was like a womb in which you were conceived, born, and raised and where you lived and married, bred and raised your children and, eventually, died. It was a world unto itself where only the old languages were still spoken. It was a state of mind, even a religion of a kind and nothing that occurred outside the Quarter could be of any interest. Inside was safety and mutual understanding and sympathy and order. All four of the men now knew, it was a world that no longer existed, and would never do so again.

* * *

The sombre mood began to dissipate as Christmas grew closer, but of course, it recalled a whole host of memories. Gathered in the mess before turning in for the night Jan suddenly began to speak his thoughts.

"About now, at home, we used to decorate our Christmas tree in the dining room. The tree dominated the whole house with the smell of fresh pine. Setting up and decorating it was one of our greatest pleasures. Unfortunately, being human beings and greedy, much of the goodies and fruit bought for decoration were consumed by those supposed to be putting them on the tree. Despite all of this it still looked beautiful, especially after all the candles had been lit.

"We waited until we could see the first star in the sky and this was the sign that the traditional Christmas Eve supper could begin. We sat at a large table covered first of all with a layer of hay, over which was spread the tablecloth. The hay was a symbol to remind us that the Christ child also had hay in His crib as His first bedding. Before starting the meal we all took a portion of blessed bread, wishing everyone the compliments of the season. After supper we exchanged presents. We spent the time until nearly midnight singing old time Christmas carols. Then we all went to Midnight Mass in a crowded church. The ringing of bells could be heard from the sleigh travelling over the newly fallen snow." His description was greeted by total silence as the listeners remembered their own Christmas routines.

* * *

TEN

No-one was more aware of the fact that all good things come to an end than the officers and men of the *'Eagle'*, and shortly after the New Year break in 1940 they found themselves back aboard their beloved submarine. It took some getting used to. For the first time since Tallinn it was fully equipped with a total complement of torpedoes, new instruments, up-to-date charts and brand new mess furniture. Unfortunately, it was still without a main gun for the breech, removed by the Estonians in Tallinn, which could not be replaced in time. The cramped conditions remained however, and came as a bit of a shock after the spaciousness of the depot ship.

Despite the fact that it meant they were going back into action they felt it was good to be at sea again. It was their world and they had a serious job to do in hitting the enemy as hard as they could. Revenge was their only motive.

A short shake down cruise in the Firth of Forth was the prelude to their first patrol as a Royal Navy submarine. They were assigned to patrol in the North Sea off the Norwegian coast.

The weather was fine, dull, but warm, and the sea calm when they set out. It almost seemed like a pleasure cruise compared with the perilous patrols in the Baltic. At least they did not have to worry about how much water was under them.

The first alarm came two days out when Tomasz, his hand sufficiently repaired to allow him to rejoin the ship, was Officer of the Watch with Marek and two lookouts on the bridge. Marek was particularly happy because he had just glanced at his watch and seen that his replacement was due to take over the watch.

Coxswain Stefan was in the conning tower, Bosun Jacek in the control room. Signalmen, acting as lookouts, systematically searched for the troubled waters which indicated the presence of a periscope of another submarine, and scanned the horizon looking for the tell-tale smoke of a ship. They followed this with a glance around the sky looking for aircraft.

There was nothing to report.

The horizon was clear, but suddenly an object attracted the attention of one of the lookouts. The glasses of all those on the bridge swung in unison towards the area reported.

"Only a mine" they said in unison.

"It must have broken adrift from its moorings during a recent storm," said Tomasz, "and is now bouncing around on freelance activity of its own." Two seagulls flew over it and then hovered, obviously having second thoughts about landing near one of the vicious antenna sticking out of it.

Tomasz was well aware of the fact that although it was nowhere near them and not a threat, they had to get rid of it. It could not be left to float around and possibly hit another ship. After informing the Captain of his intentions, he moved the submarine closer to the mine and called up two or three seamen with rifles, preferably those who considered themselves sharpshooters. It was unlikely that they could hit one of the antennas and ignite the mine, but they could pierce the outer casing and thus sink it. It took about fifteen minutes before one of the so-called sharpshooters managed to hit the target.

"Good job it couldn't shoot back," said a cynical Tomasz, "it would have sunk us."

***

Shortly afterwards Hreinski, on the hydrophones, requested a speed reduction. Tomasz ordered 'stop engines', knowing that the hydrophone arrangements are trainable microphones outside the ship's hull which receive mechanical vibrations, and are passed to the amplifiers. The sort of vibrations can then be studied, and it is possible to deduce what sort of ship is in the vicinity. But the revolutions of the submarine's own propellers interfered with reception, so it is often essential to slow down, or stop

Hreinski soon reported that the vibrations were not those of one of the trawlers seen hanging round the previous day, the revolutions were stronger and faster.

Tomasz, looking through the periscope, reported that the fog, which had caused them to submerge earlier, had cleared and he could see a big ship - a liner.

Andras took over at the periscope and noted that as the ship had no camouflage it could well be a neutral. Cautiously he ordered the torpedo tubes loaded and trained on it, just in case.

Alarm buzzers, telephones, voice-pipes all went into action; the crew brought down to earth after their period of rest and relaxation, suddenly remembered what it can be like to be in action.

"Two ships," Andras corrected, "they look like a 15,000 ton freighter and a 3,000 ton transport. They are some distance away, but approaching."

Tomasz moved quickly to the forward torpedo room and reported the tubes cleared away, firing bottles charged, and hydraulic pumps running. He struggled to appear calm and professional, but his stomach churned with the excitement of being in action again, and the chance to use his beloved torpedoes.

Andras called out the estimated speed and direction of the

bigger of the two ships. The forward tubes were ordered to be trained on the target. At this moment they hit a snag. Using the tubes accurately was found to be impossible, as it appeared that the flooding equipment was faulty. Undeterred, Andras ordered a change to the stern tubes, and when these were on the correct bearing the compensation tanks, which enable the submarine to remain balanced when the weight of the torpedoes is released and readied, were filled.. Suddenly, there were four explosions, all lights went out and the submarine was plunged into pitch blackness, then they came on again.

"Hard a-port," ordered Andras, "down 40 metres, full speed ahead, return stern tubes to normal. It's an aircraft dropping depth charges." The idea of attacking the two vessels was abandoned.

More depth charges, and the noise of rising bubbles could be heard, then the sound of depth charges dropped away.

A nervous trembling Hreinski reported the sound of patrol vessels proceeding on the submarine's course.

Andras ordered "stop motors."

A strange noise on the hydrophones was interpreted as a buoy being dropped over them by an aeroplane. They were 40 metres down. Hreinski continued to report the sounds of propellers.

It became obvious that they were in for a long wait, so part of watch was relieved and allowed to go to crew space. Not everyone was required so there was no point in keeping them all on alert. Andras ordered the crew to limit movements and suggested that those off duty lie down so that the submarine could be kept at a stable depth. Walking about increased depth measurably, either to stern or bow. A period of quiet seemed to indicate that the patrol vessels had stopped. Silence still had to be maintained so that the submarine would not be picked up again, for the hum of the electrical pump, or even a gyro compass could reveal their whereabouts. Although gyro compasses are scarcely audibly to the ear, they can be picked up by delicate microphone detectors.

It was now a cat and mouse game with, every now and then, the searching patrol boats stopping their engines, in the hope that the submarine would think they had gone, and start up again, or rise up to periscope depth.

Enemy planes were obviously aware of their presence, for they could be picked up flying up and down the narrow fjord in line ahead, dropping depth charges from time to time. At last the noise of their explosions showed that their attacks were haphazard, sometimes close, sometimes far away.

Experience had taught them that in an attack some things, like the humidity, the dampness, the foul smelling atmosphere and difficulty in breathing, become acceptable as you get used to them, others, like the imminence of a fatal attack, eat away into the nervous system. It was impossible to accustom oneself to it all. Nervous exhaustion increases in geometric progression and eventually affects everyone.

Before long it became necessary to organise some of the crew to help clear out water which had seeped into the submarine, owing to the looseness of the cut-off of the diesel engines' exhaust. The entry of water depends on the depth. Beyond 10 metres it begins to seep in, first a few drops, then a steady flow, forced in by the pressure of water outside. Normally it can be easily pumped out, but in circumstances where the enemy is trying to locate them, the pumps cannot be used. As once before, they remembered to maintain the balance the water which had to be moved from the stern to the bow, or vice versa.

To add to the discomfort the air circulators had to be turned off so the atmosphere thickened to an uncomfortable level

Andras decided, after a long period of silence, to come to periscope depth. To do this without the aid of motors is a slow job because it is done by the hydroplanes alone, and it took nearly two hours As expected, this makes matters even worse, for it become necessary to release oxygen from the containers to freshen the air. This causes a dryness in the lungs and throat, and for some this is the worst of two evils.

Slowly the submarine rose, and the apprehension increased. At last the submarine was at periscope depth. A quick glance around showed that all was clear. The air circulators were switched on. All talk stopped, those reading put their books away.

Andras reported that the tide has swept them into the fjord and that the quays of a nearby harbour could be clearly seen.

"I wonder how we were spotted so quickly?" Andras asked no-one in particular. "How did we give our position away to the patrol boats?"

"It could have been when we tried to aim the forward torpedo tubes," suggested Piotr. "The fact something was wrong must have caused a disturbance in the surface of the water and when the periscope was raised to aim at the liner the white water wash could have given us away."

Andras nodded in agreement. He ordered the submarine to surface, and the lookouts onto the bridge. They staggered, their heads dizzy. The rapid change in the air caused buzzing in the head and pressure on ear drums, but this soon cleared. The diesels were started and the gyro compass switched on, but it would be some three or more hours before it gave a true bearing, so the ordinary compass has to be used initially.

After an hour or so the crew listening to the radio were surprised to hear that their submarine had been sunk. The Germans had claimed sinking a British submarine in the fjord in which they were trapped.

Suddenly the silhouette of a destroyer was seen on the foggy horizon and the patrol boats were out again. *'Eagle'* changes course, but so do the patrol boats, the only solution is to submerge again,

Andras had been on the bridge all night, but he immediately took up his stance by the periscope. New depth charges were heard. He ordered, "slow speed ahead, submerge to 50 metres and stop all engines."

Another major depth charge attack began, and the whole routine re-started.

The situation was accepted with resignation. It is only possible to be in a state of frightened expectancy for a limited time. Eventually the crew adopted an attitude of stoicism.

The enemy did not spare their depth charges, and their explosions constantly disturbed the water in the hope they would eventually have some luck.

Quietness returned again, the submarine stayed submerged and before long a new set of patrol vessels arrived and such was the accuracy of their approach that there was a strong feeling that they must be equipped with special anti-submarine devices. They approached the *'Eagle'*, but the depth charges were exploding too soon. The granite walls of the fjord exaggerated their sound. The water began seeping in again, and there was so much it began slopping around adding to the uneasiness among the crew. The enemy's propellers could be heard inside the submarine which was now stationary. Fear arose that bubbles caused by water leakage, or even fuel, would rise to the surface and give their position away.

The submarine was considered fairly safe at 50 metres, but the thought of so much water above them was far from comforting. Different thoughts and many prayers went through the minds of the crew, religion once again took a more important role in their lives.

"Lukasz, do you know any prayers that might get us out of this?" asks Dasay.

"There's an old Polish prayer which is a petition to Our Lady, Queen of Poland. But I never thought you had much time for that sort of thing," replied Lukasz. "It's a funny thing that people like you never think of prayer when all is going well. If God really is in His Heaven, he must have a cynical smile on his face at times like this." His message got home to many members of the crew. It was true, they only thought of praying when they were in trouble.

Tadeusz continued his constant patrolling of the submarine encouraging the men, dispensing hope and advice.

"I don't know how the hell you remain so calm and cheerful," a dejected Zygmont commented.

"I'm a fatalist old son," Tadeusz replied buoyantly. "I really don't see the point of worrying about something that might not happen. I always assume that everything will be all right and accept that unquestioningly. If something does happen then I will not be around to tell myself, 'I told you so'." He smiled broadly.

Nearby explosions concentrated the mind again, but most of the crew seemed to adopt a Tadeusz type outlook, they were largely philosophical about it, there was nothing they could do. They were in the hands of Providence.

A new series of depth charges rocked the boat. It seemed they have been set to explode at 90 metres, and the explosions were pushing the boat up every time they exploded. The philosophical silence began to become more optimistic as the sounds of detonating depth charges began to fade away. Andras took the decision to see what was going on above and reported that the coast was clear at last and the tide had carried them almost to the entrance to the fjord.

The auxiliary motors were started, supper appearedn the table, humour reappeared in conversation, but the faces showed the strain of the last few days.

Jersey, wishing to get the crew to relax, regaled them with what he was doing during the attacks.

"I have been spending some time in the radio cabin at the hydrophones. With a stop watch in my hand I estimated that the patrol boats were circling around the place where we were thought to be," he told those who would listen. "After the first irregular strong attack they dropped a depth charge, or a series of them; from each patrol boat separately, but regularly, every ten minutes. So it was quite easy to know in advance from which direction to expect the next explosions. I want you to recall the moment when the patrol vessels were steaming in the second time. The critical ten minutes were nearly over when one of them was directly over us.

"I thought I knew what was about to happen so I took off the headphones, blessed myself and consigned myself to God. I waited, looking at my stop watch, one minute passed, another patrol vessel dropped a depth charge, two minutes....three minutes.....five minutes passed before I heard the noise of its depth charges exploding. From that moment the three ships began to drop depth charges at intervals of a quarter of an hour. Why did they change their minds? I don't know. They might have wanted to spare their cans, but instead they saved us."

The way his story was greeted left doubts as to whether anyone had been listening.

* * *

ELEVEN

The voyage back to base was without incident and was largely devoted to the crew recovering their nerves, usually through aimless banter, trying to forget their most recent experience.

Piotr's main role while the *'Eagle'* was based in Rosyth had been to keep in touch with submarine headquarters, partly to understand how the Royal Navy's submarine service operated, but also to get to know the officers from other ships of the Allies based in the area.

In time he had become friendly with Lieutenant. Commander Martin Armstrong RN, his main point of contact. They got on well together, for they found they were kindred spirits, devoted sailors and professional officers with the interests of the men at heart.

On returning from their last patrol Piotr was invited by Armstrong to a cocktail party at the officers' mess in Rosyth. He had been happy to accept because it made him feel part of the bigger picture, rather than just an officer on a small foreign warship, and it would help him in his new role as a sort of liaison officer.

He still felt a stranger in a foreign land as he neared the building where he was to meet Armstrong. The feeling did not diminish when he received a warm and enthusiastic welcome from the British officer.

"Glad you could make it," Armstrong greeted him with outstretched hand.

"Happy to be invited," Piotr responded, looking around, "lot of people here."

When he arrived he was surprised, not only by the number present, but by the number of women, both WRNS officers and civilians. There was, of course, no reason why wives and girl friends should not be invited there, but it was the first time for many months that he had seen and been with so many members of the opposite sex.

"We do this two or three times a year. It gives everyone the opportunity to meet a wide range of people away from the formalities of the service, and the opportunity to gossip about other things apart from the war. It also gives us the chance to wallow in the pleasure of female company.

"There is someone I would like you to meet," he added, turning to a small group of people just behind him. He tapped a woman holding a glass of white wine, on the shoulder. She was about 1.6 metres tall, with well coiffed dark hair and was elegantly dressed in a short black dress lightened by well placed and expensive looking jewelry. She turned towards Armstrong and then saw Piotr.

"I'd like you to meet…." Armstrong started, and then stopped when he saw her expression of horror.

"What's wrong?" he asked, a look of mystified astonishment on his face. Her face had turned ashen grey as she dropped her glass. The noise of broken glass stopped the murmur of conversation that had flooded the room.

Piotr was stunned. The room around him became chaotic, a kaleidoscope of lights, faces, tables, chairs and people. His brain struggled to re-orientate itself. He could not believe what he was seeing.

"Marcia" was all he could say incredulously.

She looked as shocked and dumbfounded as he did.

"Piotr?" she asked, disbelieving.

"Do you two know each other?" Armstrong asked, bewildered

"Yes, I think so," Piotr replied. "She's my wife."

The three of them stood looking at each other not knowing what to say next. Piotr could not take his eyes off the woman standing in front of him. His mind flashed from incident to incident, the receipt of the letter, the anger he felt, the hurt, then hatred then, much later, growing concern as to what had happened to her in German-occupied Poland. A feeling that was accentuated as bad news from Poland came flowing in. Despite what she had done, he had been desperately worried about her. She was a woman he had a thought of angrily, but could not forget.

Marcia looked back at him, speechless. 'What can I possibly say?' flashed through her tangled mind.

Armstrong was embarrassed by the scene they had created, and the attention it was now receiving from those around. His own mind was confused. He tried to remember what had happened in the past, how he had met Marcia, what she had said about her husband, what had been his thoughts at the time.

Marcia too, was struggling with recollections of what had happened. Where had Piotr been when she met Martin? How had she felt at the time? What made her write the letter she sent to her husband? What had her real feelings about Martin been? How the hell should she handle this crisis?

The crash of glass and the emotion-ridden scene had now attracted the attention of most of the people in the room, and they had turned and were eyeing the scene with interest.

"I think we should go somewhere and talk," Armstrong said gently, trying to work out where they could go. A friend of his, sitting in an obscure corner with three colleagues, sensing that something unusual was taking place, signalled that they would move to his table.

The three people embroiled in the event moved towards the table, the rest of the room turned away, picked up their conversations, but kept an eye on what was happening in the corner. On the face of it all went back to normal.

"I'm not sure what to say," Armstrong said when they had sat down.

"An explanation would be helpful," said Piotr looking at Marcia, but trying not to sound too bitter. Marcia returned his look, her face still pale and expressionless, her mouth was open, but no sound came out.

"I should perhaps tell you what I know," said Armstrong placatory. "Marcia and I met

when I was the British Naval Attaché in Warsaw. I knew she was married, but I also understood that it was over, and that she was separated from her husband. I knew that he was somewhere at sea. I had fallen in love with her almost on sight, so I'm afraid I did not give much thought to you," said Armstrong, looking at Piotr.

"We started what people would call a liaison, but it was much more serious for me. When war became inevitable I was recalled to London. I knew it was impossible for me to leave Marcia to her fate. I told my superior officers that she was my fiancée and that we planned to marry, and the situation was in so much chaos at the Embassy that I got permission to let her come with me. It would never have happened in normal circumstances. I think everyone just wanted to get out. I was posted to the Admiralty in London, I requested a more active role. As I can speak five languages I was moved up here as liaison officer with commanding officers of foreign navies based here."

Piotr smiled cynically: "I was rather busy getting ready to fight a war, so I didn't know our marriage had broken down until I received Marcia's letter telling me she had found someone else, and asking for a divorce. It was news to me." He turned to Marcia: "It was a complete shock. I was shattered. It was the last thing I expected or needed at that time. I have loved you for so many years. I thought our marriage was secure."

"I'm sorry," Marcia murmured quietly.

"There's one good thing," said Armstrong cheerfully, trying to relieve the tension. "I was able to get Marcia out of the country." He left the rest of the sentence unsaid, but they all knew what the alternative might have been. It was something neither of them could deny.

"Where do we go from here?" Armstrong asked.

Piotr thought for a moment: "Nowhere," he said with emphasis. "The marriage is obviously over. There is no point in denying that. We will call it a day. Marcia can have her divorce, we'll work out the grounds later. I will be taking out a ship soon and that will need all my concentration, so as far as I am concerned this is the end." Marcia managed a cynical smile, thinking to herself that he was putting the Navy first again.

"I have to say that I am grateful and relieved that Marcia is safe, I would never have wished her any harm," he added.

"I'm sorry," Marcia repeated, still in a daze. The two men sat contemplating their drinks. It was difficult to know what more there was to say. Piotr was deep in his thoughts. Still racing through his mind was how he had been occupied with concern about Marcia in the past weeks. He had both loved and hated her, he had tried to envisage what had happened to her, who she was with, who had stolen her from him. He was pleased that she was safe, but he could not forgive the anguish she had caused him and that she had destroyed their marriage. He had no thoughts about Armstrong. There was nothing he could say to him, and there was nothing that Armstrong could say which would contribute to the situation. Whether or not he wanted to marry Marcia. That was his problem.

"I think I will go back to my ship," he said eventually. Back to the world he knew and understood.

The two men stood up, shook hands. Piotr looked at Marcia, nodded, turned and walked away.

Tomasz was on duty as Officer of the Watch when Piotr returned, and welcomed him with a cheery greeting. It was ignored as Piotr walked straight past him and went below.

"Funny bugger," thought Tomasz.

When Piotr went below he was annoyed to hear a cheerful party going on in the officers' mess. He didn't want anything to do with cheery parties, or to be cheerful with anyone, so he tried to slip past into his cabin, but Andrzej came out, bumping into him.

"Oh, you're back early . Good evening?"

"Not bad," said Piotr, "what's going on in there?" He nodded towards the rowdy mess.

"It's Jersey, having a party. He's just heard that his sister is in America. His father died shortly after we sailed, and she was smuggled out of Poland through Sweden by some very distant cousin or someone. They took her to Maine where some of the family live, so he's as happy as a sand boy. What about you?"

"It was an interesting evening," Piotr replied. "Good night."

Piotr's discovery of his wife in Rosyth depressed him, but Jersey's news that his sister was safe in America, sent general morale soaring. If they had managed to get out of Poland what about the others?

* * *

All too soon they were at sea again. Through the periscope Mucha, who was on the bridge, could see the rocky, snow-covered coast line of the Norwegian fjords which, reflected in the glassy surface of the sea, formed a pleasant, slightly indistinct picture.

The somewhat similar climatic conditions subconsciously

directed his thoughts to his native country. He described what he could see to those around him, setting off varying thoughts among the listeners, one recalling the similarity to the Polish winter, another, some of his country's traditions, others began to think again of how things were in their own towns and villages.

'*Eagle*' had been ordered to patrol off the Norwegian fjords and when they first arrived, on the surface, they had watched the coast and seen small towns and illuminated houses and cottages.

A brilliantly lit liner was heading for port, probably Bergen.

Mucha had left Eryk on the periscope with the task of making sporadic checks on what was happening He was to be called if anything came into view. After a short time the Officer Cadet reported that he could see what appeared to be a cloud of smoke on the horizon.

"It's funnel smoke" Mucha said after a quick glance, "looks like a big ship, a merchantman on a right angle course to '*Eagle*', call the Captain."

Andras took one look and ordered an immediate reduction in speed to allow the merchantman to get closer to the '*Eagle's*' course.

"The ship appears to be coming from the south-east direction, could be from Germany," reported Mucha, now back on the periscope. "It looks a bit suspicious. Let's go up and take a closer look."

The general hope among the crew was that it was a German ship so they could have a go at it. But it showed no flag.

The '*Eagle*' rose into a dull day, overcast with a cold breeze coming off the Norwegian coast. The sea was becoming slightly choppy with the white topped waves seeming to emphasise the chill in the air.

Andras ordered 'action stations' and told Piotr to organise a small boarding party. If it was a neutral ship it would have to be boarded and searched. Marcin and Tadeus were called up and six well armed sailors, some of them specialists in different languages. The plan was to stop the ship and find out what it was carrying.

"Half speed ahead, make ready the two bow tubes," Andras ordered. Tension rose as the crew began to wonder what the next move would be.

"It looks very much like a German ship," said Andras, his eyes glued to the periscope.

"Half a minute," he said suddenly, "I can read the name" he spelled it out," R-I-O

D-E J-A-N-E-I-R-O it's the 'Rio de Janeiro'. They have tried to paint out the name of the home, but it is quite clear that it is Hamburg."

"It is a bloody German," he added sharply and ordered "surface, stand by to blow ballast tanks."

The crew became almost frantic with excitement when they realised they had at last caught a German ship. 'Eagle' surfaced, and the boarding party moved onto the bridge ready for action. There was some disappointment when it became clear that the German ship was much further away than it looked through the periscope.

Zygmont was ordered to show the International Code flags "*Stop engines. The master with ship's papers is to report on board this ship immediately.*"

The effect of the signal was exactly opposite to what was expected. The German ship increased speed and turned to starboard, away from the 'Eagle', in the direction of the nearest coast line and Norwegian territorial waters.

Andras's reaction was to order 'full speed' and the 'Eagle' cut through the water at 20 knots, much faster than the prospective victim.

"We can't fire the customary shot across the bows because we haven't got a bloody gun. Let them have a machine gun burst," he ordered. Mucha, almost too excited by this first opportunity for action, gave the order for the machine gun to fire towards the ship, and they could see the bullets hitting the hull.

"It's stopping and it looks as though they are lowering a boat," Piotr reported.

Under Andras's order the *'Eagle'* turned head-on to the enemy ship pointing the torpedo tubes in her direction. The barrel of the gun was also pointed in the direction of the German ship, but of course, with no breeches, as these were taken by the Estonians and not yet replaced, it was useless. But the Germans did not know this.

Everyone on the bridge concentrated on the German crew who were slowly clambering into their boats. Mucha suggested hurrying them up with another machine gun burst, but Piotr told him sharply that it was too early for that.

"It's never too early to start shooting Germans," a hostile Mucha exploded.

"It's not getting any nearer to us," Piotr pointed out. "It is keeping its distance and it's obvious that it has no intention of slowing down."

One of the lookouts, still concentrating on his job, while everyone else has eyes only for the German ship, called out that two drifters from Norwegian coast were coming towards them.

Slawomir reported that he could pick up coded wireless messages from the German ship and it could be that they were calling up aircraft. Andras ordered another signal to the German – *'Abandon ship immediately. Intend to fire torpedo in five minutes time'.*

"He's being too bloody kind," muttered the belligerent Eryk. "I would have blown the bugger out of the water without ceremony." All the men around him nodded their agreement.

The German ship, with only a few members of the crew making lethargic attempts to escape, and with little sign of life aboard, still kept its distance from the submarine. Andras ordered Tomasz to ready number one and two torpedo tubes and agreed setting a depth of six feet as the target did not seem deeply loaded. The faint noise of water rushing into the tubes was followed by the slight customary inclination of the bow. Within seconds Tomasz reported 'torpedoes flooded'.

A dull silence prevailed among the crew below. Only the monotonous lapping of the water as the engine was stopped, and the quickening breathing of the crew, can be heard. Most of them were dwelling on thoughts of revenge. It was their first real chance to pay back the Germans and land a blow for Poland.

Minutes, seeming like an age during which nothing changed, went by and then the order 'Fire number one' was rapped out by Andras, and the crew on deck were fascinated to watch the wake of the torpedo going straight for the German ship.

A shattering explosion, a plume of fire, steam and smoke rose above the enemy ship. The dense mass of smoke expanded continuously, but now the blast of the explosion hit the submarine which rocked wildly in the blast. Unexpectedly a mass of men appeared on the deck of the German ship.

A sudden: "Where did they come from?" comes from Andras as the deck of the German ship becomes crowded with human shapes, dressed in grey green uniforms. Total panic seemed to have broken out as some of them began throwing pieces of wood into the sea and jumping in after them, fear in its extreme sense was clear for all to see.

Slowly the German ship began to heel over to starboard, and the watching Poles were ecstatic to see a gaping hole between bridge and funnel. The smoke continued to spread.

"Why so many men?" asked a mystified Tomasz. "They can't possibly be members of the crew." The extreme extent of the panic became clear when it was pointed out that they had not lowered most of the lifeboats, which remained hoist at their davits,. But hordes of men were leaping into the water.

"They've got uniforms on," shouted Eryk, looking through his glasses. "There're bloody German soldiers, hundreds of them." All glasses were now turned on the panicking men on the deck of the broken ship, and in the water. It was quite clear that they were soldiers and they were Germans.

"Aircraft approaching from the Norwegian coast," a lookout shouted.

"Diving stations!" Andras ordered: "Clear the bridge, take her down."

As the crew quickly descended into the submarine, rapid handshakes indicated the joy in their success.

"Norwegian trawlers are picking up some of the survivors," Andras noted.

"If they are German soldiers they should be left where they bloody well are. We don't want them rescued and dried out so that they can fight again," commented a blood thirsty Eryk. Most of the crew agreed with him, although Lukasz expressed the view that although they may be German soldiers, they were still human beings. This drew a snort from Eryk.

"They were not acting like human beings when they smashed their way across Poland killing men, women and children," he snapped angrily.

The most enthusiastic members of the crew were the torpedo men, proud of the fact that in their first real attack they had sunk a German ship. But the ship had refused to sink. She had heeled over to an angle of 30 degrees, but that was all.

"Her watertight doors must have been closed," observed Tabbert. "And the fact that the sea is not really rough helps."

Andras continued to watch as the trawlers slowly picked up survivors and put them back on the damaged transport. It was too far from the shore to take them all to land. They probably planned to send tugs out and tow the wreck with the survivors on board, back to the shore.

"I think we'll have to finish it off with another torpedo," Andras declared. "If they are German soldiers they must be part of an invasion force. If that's true then we want the ship and its cargo out of the way."

The crew of the *'Eagle'* applauded the idea of a second attack seeing it as avenging several Polish ships, including *'Wisher'* and *'Gryf'* which they knew the Germans had sunk shortly after the invasion

"I would suggest that it would not be right to stop the trawlers picking up survivors as they will if we fire another torpedo. And we will be throwing all those already rescued back into the sea. In these temperatures they would almost certainly die in an hour or so," said Piotr quietly.

"And if we don't attack again, the vast majority will be put ashore and be able to start killing Norwegians and doing to Norway what they have already done to Poland," Andras replied succinctly, without emotion.

"If we do as you suggest we will be just as bad as they are, killing people who cannot defend themselves. Consigning them to a horrible death," Piotr continued.

"My dear Piotr, how can you possibly say we will be as bad as they are. They are invaders attacking another set of innocent people. We are trying to stop them. This is not a game, it is a war. Unfortunately kill or be killed is a fact of life, if that's not a contradiction. I have no desire to be killed and I am going to blow the ship out of the water. It may kill a few hundred soldiers, but it might also save thousands of Norwegian lives."

"Yes, Sir," Piotr said gently. He had no wish to argue with a superior officer, even though he thought he was wrong. This was the Navy, not a debating society.

Tomasz was delighted that his team was being allowed to go back into action again and anxiously awaited the Captain's order. The second torpedo was fired and another tremendous roar announced that the torpedo had struck its target. It broke the German ship in two, the bow sinking first and the stern half, crowded with men following it quickly. Andras ordered Marek to take a photographic record of the event.

The Norwegian trawlers turned away sharply and gave up picking survivors, as they were already overloaded, and made for the shore.

Spirits on the *'Eagle'* remained high as no further help seemed to be arriving for the Germans. An aircraft flew over, but no assistance was visible.

Piotr knew that those still alive had no chance of making the coast, especially as they had not lowered all their own boats. Although some had life jackets, it was thought that they would not be able to last more than a few hours. The freezing temperature could be clearly calculated from the submarine as they scanned the snow covered coastline of Norway. He silently crossed himself, and said nothing.

Andras immediately ordered that a radio-telegram be sent to the British Admiralty reporting what had happened and the stressing the evidence that a German invasion of Norway was imminent. A similar cable was despatched to the Norwegian Government.

After an hour or so *'Eagle'* edged closer to the floating bodies. It was clearly seen that they were in military uniform so this confirmed that they could only be invading troops.

When Piotr and Mucha suggested that they should surface and bring aboard some bodies as evidence Andras pointed out that if they were already dead there was no point. And he had no intention of endangering the *'Eagle'* by surfacing and making itself a target.

The periscope was raised and it could be seen that the bodies were even closer, their life jackets keeping them afloat and together. Some, it was thought, could still be alive. But they were the enemy, perhaps they had been among those who had helped to viciously attack and destroy Poland. Little sympathy was expressed by any members of the crew, but Piotr, Mucha and the would-be priest, Lukasz, remained unhappy.

Listening to the radio that evening they heard a report, in Norwegian, which mentioned the *'Rio de Janeiro'* a few minutes later came the British news: *'At noon today a British submarine on patrol torpedoed and sank, off Lillesand on the south coast of Norway, the German supply ship 'Rio de Janeiro', a Hamburg liner which had 400 soldiers and war material on board.'*

The crew reaction was one of exaltation. The report added that later in the day another submarine had sunk a 14,500 ton German tanker.

* * *

During the night the submarine received a signal which warned that the Norwegian government was switching off all navigation lights and that there would be a general blackout in the country.

A new war?

Piotr made a quick check of the bearings of the three lighthouses in the area, just before they went out, while Andras decided to steer west as darkness fell. Just after midnight they heard the noise of several aircraft, then saw rockets being fired, then heard anti-aircraft fire followed by bursting bombs. Later they saw the blazing wreckage of the tanker attacked by another submarine.

A new war had really started.

* * *

The *'Eagle'* continued its patrol with the torpedo men still reflecting in the glory of their successful attack. But they, and the rest of the crew, were quickly reminded of the facts of wartime life when suddenly the whole inside of the ship resounded with the explosion of a depth charge.

Andras quickly swept the horizon with the telescope, pausing at one point for a moment.

"Dropped by an aircraft I think," he said," but there are some patrol boats heading towards us, probably alerted by the aircraft. Take her down to 50 metres."

The whole, and now very familiar, routine of being battered and bruised by attacks started again. Very quickly, more depth charges, more twisting and turning as the submarine was thrown about by the explosions. Glass shattered, pipes bubbled with gushing leaks, lights flickered. Andras ordered the submarine down to 80 metres. The atmosphere in the submarine became damp and unpleasant, reminding them of those desperate days in the Baltic.

But it was different. In those days when under attack all they knew was that when it was over they would still be in danger with nothing to do, but await the next attack with no real hope in the future. Now, however, they were confident that if they came through this attack they would be heading home to safety and, with a bit of luck, the comfort of the depot ship.

Another pattern of depth charges, some quite close.

The noise was ear shattering, the continuous vibrations nerve-racking. None of the crew were panicking, they took great comfort once again from their seemingly imperturbable Captain.

For two hours the German vessels unloaded over 50 depth charges adopting a system which set them at various depths. In a damp atmosphere and with only temporary lighting the crew waited silently in the midst of chaos, broken glass and water.

Henerey looked terror-stricken. Rigid, his knuckles white, as he held his valves in a vice-like grip.

"Feeling worried?" asked Tadeusz. His under-estimated question was ignored.

Tadeusz noted that Henerey's trousers were damp with urine. There was no immediate answer, but Henerey nodded without looking up.

"Thinking about those wide open spaces?"

"Thinking about these bloody depth valves and which way they are going to go," said Henerey, still glaring at the gauges.

"The worst is over," said Tadeusz gently, "we'll soon be back in port to all the problems we face there, where am I going to go to get drunk, how to spend my pay, where do I find a girl, serious things like that." He put his hand on Henerey's shoulder,

"You're doing damn well," he added.

It was with some relief that Henerey noticed that Tadeusz had walked away. Now he could go back to concentrating on his valves. It was good, he also thought, to know he was doing well.

A fresh attack, four, then five detonations. Two blows hit the boat broadside. More wild rolling, pitching and gurgling. Andras stood steady, watching the depth gauge. The rest of the crew continued to wait silently, grasping hold of anything which would enable them to remain comparatively steady.

* * *

The only way to combat the terror was to try and think about something else and once more the crew's thoughts turned to their homes and families.

Jake's thoughts, however, were on something much more mundane. His sex life.

Hreinski shuffled up to him, lying on the deck, and asked: "How did it go?"

"It was okay." Jake lied, not wishing to admit it was one of the most awful experiences he had ever had.

A few days before they last went on shore leave Jake had

asked Hreinski, knowing his reputation with women, how he got hold of them in the first place.

"Easy," Hreinski had replied cockily, "you just chat them up for a while, be nice to them, pay them compliments and you're home and dry."

"Not for me," Jake complained," it doesn't work. I can't speak English well enough, I splutter, and they think I'm funny."

"No, that should make it much easier for you," said Hreinski, adopting a serious look. "You can be more forward in telling them what you want. If they complain then you apologise because you don't know the right English words to use. That will win you their sympathy and they won't want to upset you. They'll be only too happy to let you do what you want."

"It won't work for me," said Jake sadly.

"You should try it. Anyway, if it's that important, pick up a prostitute, you don't have to play games with them. They know what you want and how to give it. It's their job. The only thing is, it will cost you."

"How much?"

"Varies, ten shillings at most, depends on what you want. They'll tell you and you don't have to do it, it will be entirely up to you."

Jake had taken his word for it, and decided it was the easiest way to get what he wanted. He still had wonderful thoughts about his first experience and wanted to repeat it as soon as possible. He set about his task with new determination. It was not needed. He did not have to go looking for a prostitute, he was propositioned immediately he started walking down a side street on the edge of the city centre.

"You want a good time?" asked a woman of medium height with a revealing skirt and big breasts. She had a plain face, not very attractive, but her breasts, which were only partly hidden by a tight blouse which was fighting a loosing battle to contain them, were very tempting.

"How much?" he had asked.

"Ten shillings for a quick one, with no extras." Jake had no idea what 'extras' might have been and ten shillings was a large proportion of his weekly pay, but why not?

"Where do we go?"

"I've got a room round the corner, come on." She led the way round the corner into a narrow street of small terraced houses. She stopped at a door that looked as though a paint stripper had left the job unfinished, up some narrow stairs into a small room with a single bed, a table which held a wash basin and jug, and a chair. Nothing else, no pictures, a dirty blind instead of curtains and a smell which seemed to be a mixture of cheap perfume and rotten food, not much better than a submarine after a few weeks at sea submerged.

"You got the money?" she asked, holding out her hand. He gave her a crumpled, dirty note. It seemed apt.

"Wash yourself," she ordered.

Jake picked up a small bar of soap and began to wash his hands in the basin.

"Not your hands, your cock. Give it a good wash." Jake was beginning to feel he had done the wrong thing, there was none of the gentle romance of his first experience. He had begun to lose his sex drive, but when she went up to the bed, took off her skirt to show she was not wearing knickers, it began to take life again. He stepped forward as if to take her in his arms and kiss her.

"No kissing. I don't do kissing." She snapped, lying back on the bed and opening her legs. "Get on with it," she instructed. Jake took off his trousers and was pleased to see that his equipment was working despite the lack of foreplay. He climbed on the bed and thrust his penis into her. He felt the damp warmth of his previous experience, but it was clearly a well used highway, there was none of the tight grip he had expected.

She lay prone and unmoving as he gently thrust himself into her and there was no reaction when he felt himself coming to climax. The moment he finished she thrust him off her. She put her skirt back on and waited while he dressed and then showed him the door.

Jake had stood outside the door completely disillusioned and unclean. Is that what it was usually like? Was his first experience unusual? He had been physically satisfied, was mentally disgusted. Never again, he thought, he felt as though he should wash himself again. He promised himself it was something he would never repeat.

His reverie was cruelly ended with a series of more explosions, but much further away. After another ten minutes, another burst. Even more distant. Then, nothing.

"Take her up to periscope depth," ordered Andras after a further half hour of silence, and then:. "Up periscope." Another quick look round.

"We are alone," he declared. "Let's go home"

* * *

The crew of the *'Eagle'* learned, when they returned to Rosyth, that the British Government had not taken much notice of their cabled warning.

During a visit to headquarters Andras was told that the ship they sank had been on its way from Hamburg to Bergen with 400 German infantry soldiers and artillery.

"It's quite incredible," he told his officers, "that the Chief of the local police in Norway had immediately sent the information that he obtained from the rescued German soldiers to the staff of the Norwegian fleet in Oslo. This was the first real confirmation of the German invasion of Norway. He was then advised to speak to the General Staff, but the general to whom he spoke explained that he was too busy to study the report and hung up.

"What is even more remarkable is that this occurred when German preparations were known to some Scandinavian diplomats and military attachés in Berlin, as well as, for example, the Norwegian legations in Copenhagen and in Berlin," he said.

"Most of the British home fleet was despatched to the Denmark Strait between Iceland and Greenland, to watch for German warships on their way to the North Atlantic to attack British convoys. And the German operations had been so coordinated that the invasion of Norway was to begin simultaneously along the whole coast.

"Therefore, even if the Norwegians had taken the reports from the German survivors more seriously, little could have been done to change the progress of the invasion," he explained, with disbelief in his voice.

"The only saving grace is that the Norwegian Government may have been warned by London, which led the mobilisation and black-out orders given on the evening of 8 April and the escape of the Norwegian Royal Family. But otherwise it was too late, the invasion began early the next day."

* * *

TWELVE

After several weeks in the Baltic battlefield, and the strain of constantly being in action, 24 hours each day, the *'Eagle's'* arrival in the Firth of Forth after an active patrol was an amazing contrast. The sight of the Scottish, and therefore friendly, coast, the presence of so many compatible warships, and the beauty of the countryside on either side felt like a cosy blanket around the crew.

The feeling of hope, which was boosted by the news of Piotr's wife and Jersey's sister, and the resulting illogical optimism about the fate of their loved ones and relatives, was intensified when they heard that Jan, Slawomir's deputy, had received a message from the Polish Embassy in London. The caller had wanted identification for a prisoner the Americans held in custody.

"What's it all about ?" Jake asked the question that was on everyone's lips.

Jan was almost too excited to talk, but managed to explain that the Americans had in custody a young Polish youth, who wore a German uniform, and had been arrested after being found stowed away on an American aircraft which had taken off from Warsaw. The boy said he was really Polish and that his father was in the Polish Navy and on the submarine *'Eagle'*. He had told them that when the Germans arrived he had been conscripted into the German army and sent with his unit to Warsaw. While there he was sent to deliver a message at another post, and had managed to do a runner and eventually get into an aerodrome near Warsaw. There was considerable confusion on the airfield and, as he was in a German uniform, no-one questioned him. At night he managed to get into the cargo hold of a plane he thought was British, but turned out to be American. It had taken off shortly afterwards, and he had nearly died through the cold and lack of air. He was unconscious when the plane landed at Northolt near London, and he was arrested.

"They asked me if I had a son," Jan explained, "and I told them I had two. They asked their names so I told them Josep and Mikolai. Then they asked me which was the eldest and I said Josep was nearly 18. They then asked me to describe him, so I told them he was around 1.5 metres, had black hair and blue eyes Had he got any distinguishing features, they asked, and I was able to describe the small birthmark he had on his right thigh. At the end of it they seemed satisfied that he was who he said he was," Jan added excitedly.

"What happens now?" asked Dasay who was among the small crowd which had gathered round, enthralled.

"He is being handed over to the Polish Embassy to decide what to do with him. I hope they'll send him to join the Polish Navy and will probably be posted up here in Rosyth," said Jan, more pleased to know that he was safe than to worry about his immediate future.

"They might send him up here to join one of our ships, or send to him to a place where they mend clocks!" Hreinski suggested.

"That would be too good to be true, But he doesn't know anything about clocks, like me they used to drive him mad," said Jan laughing.

* * *

Slawomir listened to this excited exchange, but he was almost uncontrollable with delight, because he had been ordered to report for a second medical examination. He had been briefly examined in the general health check of the whole crew when they had arrived in Rosyth, and he had been able to complain about his inability to put on weight whatever he ate. It had always been the same, he told the doctor, so he realised he must have some sort of wasting disease. His delight was that they had obviously listened to him, taken him seriously, and were now about to come up with a solution.

"You've been making fun of me ever since I told you, but now you know that I have been right all along," he said triumphantly to anyone who would listen.

"For Christ's sake shut up," said an unsympathetic Dasay. "We've heard everything a thousand times. If you've got a wasting disease then I'm pregnant."

"There's been talk about that too," muttered Guayne

Slawomir was gone for over half an hour, and when he returned the elation had vanished, his world had collapsed and his face with it.

"What happened?" asked Marek, his shock at Slawomir's appearance persuading him to show some sympathy.

"Ignorant bastards," snapped Slawomir. "They know bugger all."

"What don't they know?" asked an amused Dasay. "What did they say?"

"It wasn't a 'they'," replied the injured man, "it was a bloody he, the bloody base Medical Officer. He asked me how tall I was, which was a bloody silly question because they had checked my height at the first medical. Anyway, I said I was just over two metres which is why I have to stoop everywhere on the boat. The silly sod then asked me how much I thought I weighed and why was I so worried about it. I told him I weighed only about 80 kilograms and with my height it should be more."

"And what did he say then?" asked an engrossed Dasay, unable to stand the growing tension.

"The silly bugger said I actually weighed 95 kilos which meant I was about 10 kilos overweight and I should lose some of it, if I wanted to be healthy. Can you bloody well believe it! Me, overweight!" said a shocked Slawomir.

"We believe it, that's why we call you fatty, you dimwit," laughed Dasay.

"You do it because it's the usual senile joke, you call tall people 'shorty' and short people 'lofty' and hairy people 'baldy'."

"We should call you 'brainy' then," Dasay summed up.

Slawomir was inconsolable and drifted away, almost in tears.

* * *

After nearly a month, in the confined space of the submarine, Andras was basking in the luxury of his own comparatively spacious cabin. He saw little of his crew on a daily basis, as they were dispersed on training courses or various duties. It was only when he carried out his weekly 'Captain's Rounds' of inspection of the *'Eagle's'* quarters that he saw all of them. It was during one of these that he was approached by Kacek.

"May I have a word Sir?" asked the deferential sailor.

"Of course," replied Andras, "got a problem?"

"Well Sir. You know when we arrived here the base Medical Officer examined Lieutenant Tomasz's hand and suggested I had done a good job and that I should go for medical training?" Andras nodded. "But, I said I would rather stay with the *'Eagle'* with my friends."

"Very commendable," said his Captain, "but I thought at the time that you ought to have given it more thought."

"Well, that's it Sir, I have given it more thought and

would like to change my mind and go on a course, if it's not too late."

"It's certainly not too late. What brought about the change?"

"It was watching Lieutenant Tomasz. I got a lot of satisfaction out of seeing him use his hand almost normally. It meant I had actually done something useful. Helping people suddenly seemed worthwhile."

"Good for you," said Andras, patting his shoulder. "I'll get Lieutenant Piotr to arrange it. You'd like to transfer as soon as possible, before we sail I assume?"

"Yes, Sir, thank you."

As he was leaving the Captain, feeling happy and satisfied, he was given a further boost by Hreinski.

"You performed a bloody miracle on my cock," he said.

"You mean it has grown into a proper sized cock, or it hasn't dropped off?"

"It's a damn sight better than it was, thanks to you." He didn't explain which of the alternatives he was talking about.

"I've been examined again by the doc and everything is back to normal, and he said that there was no sign of a disease of any sort. It was that stuff you gave me to soak it in that did it. What was it, the thing you said was a secret family recipe?"

"Vinegar."

"No! really?"

"Really. Plain old vinegar."

"How did you know vinegar would do it?"

"I didn't. It was the only thing I'd got. I heard my father talk about vinegar once, but I think he was putting it on his food. Anyway, it worked."

"Certainly did, thanks"

"Think nothing of it."

For the first time for weeks Kacek felt that life was very good.

* * *

The German invasion of Norway was in full swing, and there were constant rumours about when the *'Eagle'* would be sent back into action. It was known that one reason for any delay was the fact that the main gun was, at last, being replaced and was occupying most of Chief Gunner Mucha's time.

Rumours came to a head when a ship's company meeting was called to be held in the seamen's mess on the depot ship.

"He's going to announce a sailing date," declared Jake.

"Don't be bloody silly," responded Dasay, "you don't announce a sailing date in wartime. You creep out secretly without telling anyone."

"No, he's going to give us the latest news from Poland," said a despondent Guayne.

"You mean the latest news about your dog," offered Dasay.

"No you useless prick," Guayne responded.

"What do you think?" Tomasz asked Piotr quietly.

"I honestly don't know, he hasn't confided in me and that's unusual. It could be something about Poland."

Andras was quick to put everyone's mind at rest when he started speaking.

"You all know how proud I am of this crew. Your courage, determination, resolve, fortitude and stoicism is unequalled in Polish Navy history. You have all been magnificent.

"Our strength has been the fact that we are a closely knit team, everyone dependant on and helping each other no matter what rank. But, as the British have a habit of saying, all good things come to an end. Our purpose in life is to fight on behalf of Poland, not just keep up our own cosy existence. We have to make changes.

"The bad news for most of you is that I am to remain as Captain, confirmed in the rank of Commander," there was a murmur of approval. "But Lieutenantt Piotr, who is promoted to Lieutenant Commander is being given his own ship, a Polish destroyer," more murmurs of agreement, "while the three Officer Cadets, Eryk, Marek and Yarwin, will be posted to other ships to broaden their experience." This was greeted by a small cheer as the three men concerned looked at each other with doubtful expressions.

"There are some other well deserved promotions. Chief Petty Officer Artor is being considered for a commission, and will go to the Royal Navy's training school on the south coast, Petty Officer Marcin stays on the *'Eagle'*, but as Chief Petty Officer, while Leading Seaman Jake becomes a Petty Officer, and will also remain on board. The well known medical genius Kacek is going to the Royal Navy medical school in Portsmouth. All those who have been treated by him and wish to complain or take legal action should form a queue along the jetty."

Andras also revealed that 13 other crewmen, mainly the older ones, would be given other postings, but the only one of the lower deck postings he mentioned was Henerey.

"Seaman Henerey has been under particular strain in the past weeks with serious problems due to an abnormal fear of confined spaces, a medical condition called claustrophobia. He has not confessed this to anyone as far as I know," Andras explained much to Henerey's horror. He thought only Tadeusz knew about his problem.

"He has done his work in an exemplary manner," Andras continued, "but it is considered that he would be even more efficient in a posting ashore or on a larger surface ship." All eyes were turned on Henerey, but the looks were those of respect and sympathy, unseen by Henerey, who had lowered his head in embarrassment.

"All those who have been posted will be leaving in two days' time. I am extremely sorry to lose you all, but I wish you all success and hope that one day we can meet after our victory."

With a boisterous outbreak of conversation and speculation the meeting ended. Those leaving had mixed emotions. The *'Eagle'* had been their home, and the crew their family. They were going into an unknown world, in a foreign country with people they did not know, and a future even more uncertain.

* * *

Shock and surprise were two adjectives which could be used to describe Piotr's and the Officer Cadets' reaction.

Although nothing had been said, Piotr knew that he had to thank Andras for his promotion. It was unexpected because he knew how important it was to keep good, experienced submarine crews together. But when he had got over the initial shock, he allowed a feeling of pride to sink in. To actually command his own ship, and a destroyer at that, and as a Lieutenant Commander, was something of which he could really be proud. He had no doubts that he could do the job, he had had a good teacher, and he had a few ideas of his own.

It had certainly been an amazing six months. He had lost a wife, been engaged in a war, taken part in an exciting escape from Tallinn, and then from the Baltic, got to Britain and freedom, found his wife and lost her again, helped sink a German troopship and discovered Germany's invasion of Norway, and now promotion and a command, What could happen next?

The proudest man was probably Chief Petty Officer Artor, his dream of promotion was opening up before him. He would have to pass exams and there was always the problem that he was a man of action, not a great original thinker. But, he could learn, at least, he thought he could.

No-one was more surprised than Petty Officer Marcin on being promoted to Chief. He thought that stealing a superior officer's girl friend and then fighting him over it had put an end to his promotion prospects for ever. Maybe it was what he did for Tomasz and, according to the Captain, for the submarine that had helped. But he knew from experience that one action did not make a career. His thoughts were interrupted by Tomasz himself.

"Congratulations, you deserve it," he said, patting him on the back. "You probably think it has something to with what you did for me and the ship, but you would be wrong. It had much to do with the fact that you are good sailor, good at your job and good with the men."

"Thank you Sir," was all Marcin could think to say. He could not remember ever being embarrassed before.

Tadeusz moved toward the humiliated Henerey, and urged him to the side of the room.

"You have nothing at all to be ashamed of," he said in a low voice. "Most of us agree that you have been the bravest member of this crew. We are all probably too clueless to understand how near to death we have been during the past weeks, but you knew, you were terrified most of the time, yet you did your job without failing. I am extremely proud of you and you should be extremely proud of yourself."

"Quite right," said Tomasz, who had walked up while Tadeusz was speaking.

"Everyone agrees."

Henerey, tears welling up in his eyes could only say "Thank you."

Jake thought his promotion was a joke. "Me! A Petty Officer?" They must be mad.

"You owe me a month's pay," Dasay interrupted his thoughts.

"What the hell for?" asked a shocked Jake.

"I bet you a month's pay you would be promoted if ever we got to Britain."

"Like hell you did," snapped Jake, "When?"

"When we were off Bornholm, just after we dropped off the

Estonians. It's no use arguing, I've got witnesses," replied Dasay, nodding towards Guayne, Henerey and Hrienski who all showed their agreement.

"You are a bunch of lying bastards," said Jake with increasing incredulity. "I don't remember the subject even being discussed. And you would not even bet a month's pay on your Mother being a woman. You're a mean sod. Anyway, you haven't any proof."

"I think I've got a piece of paper with it written down." said Guayne, fiddling in his pockets. Jake was getting worried, trying hard to remember whether any such a bet was ever laid among all those he made with the crew.

Guayne continued fiddling while the others watched with serious expressions. But a smile, which he could not control, developed and turned into a laugh. All the others started laughing.

"Perhaps you'll be a bit more careful about what bets you make in the future," said a collapsing Dasay.

"You rotten sods," was Jake's contribution as he joined in the laughter.

* * *

There was a strange atmosphere in the *'Eagle's'* quarters of the depot ship following the meeting. For those who could remember it, there was a strong resemblance to the last day of term at school. The leavers were full of excitement, those remaining wanted to get the changes over and get back to sea, to a world and routine they were used to.

There was general approval of the promotions that had been announced, although Jake got a lot of piss-taking, to which he responded with jocular use of his new authority, ordering Guayne to stop talking about his bloody dog and tidy up his locker, Dasay to moderate his language, and Hreinski to change his morals. All three told him to go and get stuffed.

Jersey was allowed 48 hours leave to meet up with his brother, Kacek was immediately despatched to the Royal Naval Hospital at Haslar near Portsmouth, while Artor was given a railway pass to take him to the Officers Training Establishment at Hove on the south coast of England.

The final day before sailing was spent packing kit and saying goodbyes.

Everyone who was able, without duties, took advantage of the shore leave. Last shopping was done – fruit: fresh, dried and tinned, they could never get enough. Bread and cigarettes, although it was only possible to smoke for short periods. Of course, not when a submarine was submerged, but only in the diesel compartment when on the surface, although the rolling boat on the surface often put people off lighting up. When in harbour some members of the crew usually smoked two or three times as much. They also brought aboard, tidbits of food and writing paper, Most of their gear was left in the depot ship including photo albums, old letters and souvenirs.

The uncertainty ended suddenly with an announcement that there would be shore leave until 2000 that night and the submarine would be casting off early the next morning. It was a welcome relief.

It was 0530 the next morning when the *'Eagle'* cast off and made its way down the Firth of Forth under a cloudless sky, and the light of a three-quarter moon reflecting on a choppy sea, slightly agitated by a strengthening breeze.

"Good to be back at sea," said Officer of the Watch Tomasz to his Captain standing next to him.

"At last," Andras replied with enthusiasm, "I couldn't stand much more of the officialdom and routine of life on the base. Let's see what the future has to offer us."

* * *

EPILOGUE

Silence.

Total silence.

A silence so intense it made the nerves tingle. Only the breathing of those gathered in the wireless room, which became faster as the silence extended, gave the scene any semblance of life.

Several chalk-white faces stared intensely at the speaker on the equipment, willing it to produce a noise, any sort of noise that indicated there was life at the other end.

"Give it another go," demanded an authoritative voice.

The operator tapped out the *Eagle's* call sign and, after thirty seconds, repeated it.

Nothing.

Piotr, who had been at the base HQ finalizing arrangements to take over his destroyer, had been called to the wireless room by his Royal Navy friend Armstrong. The Englishman's face was dark and unsmiling.

"It's not good news I'm afraid. It looks as though the *Eagle* is missing. We have lost contact with her. She could not be raised at her usual check in time."

"Could be a radio problem," said Piotr hopefully. "It's not unknown."

"Yes, could be, but I should tell you that German radio has

reported sinking a British submarine in the North Sea, in an area where the *'Eagle'* should have been.

Piotr's body went icy cold. He could not believe what he was hearing. He had heard bad news before, but however bad it had been, he always had an instinctive gut feeling that everything would turn out all right. It had always proved to be so. The trouble was that this time the deep feeling of optimism was missing

He tried to tell himself that a twinge of optimism was really there, but in his heart he knew that things were as bad as they could be.

"Where was she?" he asked Armstrong.

"Somewhere near Bergen, off the Norwegian coast. She had picked up a German convoy on its way to the port. The German report just said a submarine had been sunk in that area. It didn't say how it was supposed to have happened, through depth charges from aircraft, or escorts, or a mine or whatever," Armstrong sighed hopelessly.

"Not much doubt then?"

"Afraid not."

Piotr looked at the radio in despair. In his mind he reviewed what could have happened. It might really be a troublesome radio, they had no alternative means of communication if it didn't work. There had been several instances when a ship reported lost in action had suddenly turned up explaining that they could not signal that they were okay. But that German radio report? Well, they were always reporting fictitious sinkings.

The *'Eagle'* had been reported sunk in the Baltic when they escaped from Tallinn, and again afterwards. So it might be all right.

But it wasn't, Piotr knew it.

The *'Eagle'* had gone and everyone aboard had been killed. But how did it happen?

Was it a mine or a depth charge which destroyed the submarine and the whole crew with one devastating blow? Or was it just fatally damaged and lying on the bottom with some of the crew still alive?

Piotr hoped it was the former, the alternative was too awful to contemplate. But he knew that if this was so, his good friend Andras, if he was still alive, would have tried to maintain calm with the help of the ever cheerful, ever optimistic Tadeus. But would they have to maintain calm? The crew of the *'Eagle'* would not panic, they were not the sort, they would be composed and philosophical. Jake would probably re-start his conversation about death, unless he had already found the answer. And he would probably try to start a book, betting on their chances of escape. Dasay would be complaining about everything not meaning a word of it, and would be just as strong and controlled as the others.

Guayne would be worrying about who would look after his dog, Tomasz and Marcin would certainly be cementing their new-found friendship, and be agreeing what a meaningless waste of time their argument had been. Jersey would be regretting that he was not able to say goodbye to his sister and would start worrying again that she would now really be alone.

Piotr thought of his long term friend Mucha, the former schoolteacher, and the life they had known together. He was not sure what his reaction would be, but it certainly would not be panic, he would be keen to set an example. Lukasz would be praying like mad, sure that he was about to meet his Maker. Jacek and Ryzard would be seriously discussing possible steps towards escape, knowing full well that there was no chance, but giving hope and confidence to those listening.

He remembered the scarcely concealed excitement of Marcin and Jake at their promotions. He wondered how the three Officer Cadets, the cheerful Eryk, the serious Marek, and the nervous Yarwin, and Artor and Kacek would react to the news. They, like him, would have a desperate feeling of horror, mixed with a feeling of guilt that it had not happened while they were with their colleagues.

He reflected on the difficulties they had all come through, the crawl through the minefield, the escape from Tallinn, the desperate depth charge attacks, the breakout through the Sound, the sinking of the Rio de Janeiro. For what? And why, oh why, should he be the one to escape?

*　*　*

A desolate Piotr looked around him at naval colleagues who understood his distress, but had no words to help ease his pain. He should leave, he told himself, to save them embarrassment and to clear his mind.

"I'm going for a walk," was all he said as he left the room and went out into the dull, cloudy day. 'Thank God the sun isn't shining', he thought.

A walk out of the dockyard, even though it would provide a number of reminders about the recent past, seemed the answer. He thought of going for a drink in one of the pubs, but felt sure that someone he knew would be there and would want to talk

He walked towards the gates where his attention was attracted by two women standing there talking and studying a piece of paper. They were clearly not the sort of women who normally hung round the gates. The tall one was well dressed, showing a good sense of taste, while her companion was smaller, but equally attractive, Piotr noticed that both women had black hair, and neither used makeup.

"Excuse me," said the taller one approaching him. "I wonder whether you can help us." He noticed that there was a hint of a foreign accent.

"I will try," he replied politely, annoyed that his solitude was being interrupted.

"We are looking for the Polish submarine *'Eagle'*." A shiver of apprehension went through Piotr, "which we've been told it is based here. My husband is the First Lieutenant and this lady's husband, Andrzej, is an officer."

Piotr's first reaction was that they were imposters. He was the *'Eagle's'* First Lieutenant. His mind was in a confused whirl as he tried to understand what was going on. Once again belief was suspended.

He studied the woman who was totally mystified by his reaction. Then realisation began to dawn on him. It could not be. It was too difficult, and too awful to believe.

"We were trapped in Poland, but were helped to escape by a wonderful pro-Jewish group" she explained. "We have been in England two days and the Polish Embassy in London suggested we should come up here. They said the *'Eagle'* was based here."

Piotr looked at the two women, not knowing what to say or how to break the news. Eventually he managed to stammer a reply.

"Alekzandra?" he asked uncertainly.

"Yes," was her surprised response. "I am Andras's wife. Do you know him?" she asked.

"Andras was the *'Eagle's'* Captain, Andrzej was one of his officers," he replied, speaking Polish.

"You are Polish?" she asked incredulously.

And then she noticed: "Was?"

"Yes," he replied gently. "I think we should go somewhere and talk."